The Latin Heart of English

English vocabulary practice of words of Latin origin

Volume 1

Marc Loewenthal

Liondale Publications
132A Heather Park Drive
Wembley
Middlesex HA0 1SN
http://www.eflworksheets.com
marcolo@supanet.com

The Latin Heart of English
English vocabulary practice of words of Latin origin
Volume 1

ISBN 978-0-9558484-2-1

Contents

5

Introduction

Vocabulary is an integral and fundamental part of any language learning programme. There are numerous ways for learners to expand their vocabulary, including associating words in semantic fields, making spider-grams, writing lists, practising affixation and identifying collocations. Another effective method is presenting and practising words derived from the same root, which helps learners to see relationships in form and meaning. This book extends this idea by selecting some of the most important roots in Latin to act as the focus for studying their derivations together, mainly through comparing their meanings and practising affixation.

The main reason for using Latin roots as the focus is that they form the basis of the major part of modern English vocabulary, especially the type of vocabulary that students need to learn in order to progress to more advanced levels. Another reason is that Latin provides a rich variety of prefixes and suffixes which work together with the roots to produce new vocabulary. This book provides a unique opportunity for students of English not just to learn important new vocabulary, but also to examine how words are formed and to generalise across the roots how affixes create and change meaning.

The book consists of explanatory notes on the history of Latin words in English, notes on pronunciation and prefixation, explanatory notes on the roots, and a hundred exercises practising over one thousand words. It is hoped that after completing all the exercises in this book, students will have a much greater command of vocabulary and a greater sense of how to interpret and deduce new vocabulary. Two more volumes are planned to cover other important Latin roots. For further information and more exercises and activities, visit http://www.eflworksheets.com.

A short history of Latin words in English

In these notes, original Latin root words are given in bold, e.g. **agere**, modern English derivations are given in italics, e.g. *agenda*, and meanings are given in speech marks, e.g. "drive".

Historically, at its height in the 2nd C CE, the Roman Empire stretched from Britain to Palestine, and Latin was spoken as its official language. Latin, like English, is a descendent of the Indo-European family of languages. By the 6th C CE, the modern descendents of Latin - French, Spanish, Portuguese, Italian and Romanian (as well as Catalan, Sardinian and many other dialects) - had started to form as separate languages from the Latin vernacular. As these languages developed, vocabulary was altered both in meaning and pronunciation, especially in French.

In the 6th C CE, Germanic tribes began to settle in Britain, and brought with them the language which eventually became modern English. The dialects spoken by the first settlers were closely related to those spoken in modern Holland, Northern Germany and the Frisian Islands. Throughout its history, English has absorbed words from other languages. Old English even brought Latin and Greek vocabulary with it from Germany, such as *butter, cheese* and *cheap*. With the arrival of Christianity, many Latin and Greek words were borrowed and absorbed by English to such an extent that many are not immediately recognisable as borrowings. These include ecclesiastical vocabulary like *bishop, church* and *parish*, as well as other words like *port, temple* and *candle*.

The next large-scale borrowing of vocabulary came from the Norse and Danes, who settled in Scotland and much of the north of England. They spoke dialects related to English, and may have even been able to communicate reasonably well with the English speakers, supplying words like *egg, scream, take* and *get*. However, the next great influx of words forms the bulk of modern English vocabulary, ironically from a people who were originally Norse, but who lost their Norse language.

The Normans had settled along the coast of Northern France in the 8th and 9th centuries, but they very quickly lost their native language and took on French, although they spoke a dialect different from standard French. In 1066, William, Duke of Normandy, invaded England and defeated Harold, the English king. From that point, England was gradually taken over by the French-speaking Normans, with the result that English was largely reduced to the language of the lower classes, while Norman French was the language of the ruling classes. Over the next 200 years, as the ruling classes began to identify themselves more with their English subjects than with the increasingly foreign French, English began to reassert itself. However, many everyday words in Old English were lost in the transition to Middle English, as huge quantities of French words came into standard usage. We can see this clearly in the works of writers like Geoffrey Chaucer.

By the 15th C, Middle English had accumulated a huge number of French words, as well as a large number of words borrowed from Latin (either directly or through French), which had remained the main language of learning. This list gives some examples of words borrowed from French: *achieve, affair, asset, cattle, chief, city, close, damage, defeat, despise, double, dress, fail, gentle, grief, join, lieu, maintain, please, point, power, print, prison, prize, push, rail, relieve, reply, rest, royal, saint, second, sense, sever, sign, size, sport, spouse, stage, sure, survive, tense, trail, treat, trouble, very, void*.

Since then, English has continued to accumulate Latin vocabulary, mainly through the Renaissance and also through new creations and discoveries in science and technology, including the following: *agent, capital, concrete, donation, dual, fact, finite, fracture, general, local, memory, minor, nature, person, progress, reside, solve, spectator, spectrum, status, tractor* and *vacate*. In fact, while the core vocabulary of English descends from the original Germanic, the vast majority of words in English have their ultimate origins in Latin.

While many derivations have come straight from Latin, most have passed through French. As a result, their forms have been significantly altered to the extent that they may no longer be recognisable as coming from the original Latin root. In addition, two derivations may exist, one from Latin (sometimes directly, sometimes via Old or Middle French), and another from French (substantially altered from the original Latin). In these cases, the meanings may be more or less similar, and they may be used in different ways, with different levels of formality and different collocations. Here are some examples:

rex, "king"
→ *regal* (from Latin via Old French)
→ *royal* (from Old French)

vox, "voice"
→ *vocal* (from Latin via Old French)
→ *vowel* (from Old French)

securus, "safe"
→ *secure* (from Latin)
→ *sure* (from Old French)

jungere, "join"
→ *junction* (from Latin via Old French)
→ *joint* (from Old French)

pungere, "pierce"
→ *puncture* (from Latin via Old French)
→ *point* (from Old French)

caput, "head"
→ *capital* (from Latin via Old French)
→ *chief* (from Old French)
→ *chef* (from Modern French)
→ *captain* (from Latin through Old French)
→ *chieftain* (from Old French).

How students can benefit

It is hoped that these activities will be useful and stimulating to students of English whose first language is a Romance language. They can be particularly useful to them in comparing forms and uses across the two languages and within English, in particular the differences and similarities in meanings and uses, e.g. *sensitive* compared with *sensible*, as well as revealing "false friends" (similar words with different meanings), e.g. English *actual*, "real, true", compared with French *actuel*, "present, current". Such learners may not have a clear idea of these meanings and uses, and these materials are designed to help students fix the meanings and uses more firmly in their minds. However, those learners whose first language is not a Romance language will also find these exercises useful in helping them understand the complex and rich mix of vocabulary, affixations, derivations and meanings of English vocabulary. At the same time, these exercises can stimulate in them an interest in investigating the history and nature of the English language further. Latin teachers, in addition, may find this book gives their students a clearer understanding of Latin vocabulary and its importance in the development of Modern English.

Regarding the ELT level of these materials, they range from Intermediate to Advanced, though teachers should judge how suitable each exercise would be for their students. It may be best to use these materials to reinforce vocabulary work done from a course book, especially in preparation for an exam. Students can be given them for homework, or can work on them together in class and share their ideas. Alternatively, individual exercises can be used to expand on points which come up in class. The notes on pronunciation, prefixes and the exercises are designed to guide teachers, though they can also benefit students who want to gain a more detailed knowledge of word formation and meaning.

Notes on pronunciation, prefixation and the exercises

The notes below give the approximate pronunciation of the Latin roots and the meanings of the most common prefixes, and also highlight meanings and features of the original Latin roots. They also discuss any aspects of the derivations that might not be immediately apparent. Each one is meant only as a guide and not as a detailed explanation of each root.

In the exercises, the derivations are mainly nouns, verbs or adjectives, and occasionally adverbs, so the learner should think about the type of word that should go into a gap according to the grammar and syntax of the sentence. In many cases, this means changing a verb to another form and putting a noun in the plural. In some exercises, the same derivation is used twice, indicated by *(2)* after the derivation. In most of these cases, the derivation is used as two different parts of speech, for example, a noun and a verb as with *voice*. In a few of these cases, the forms differ in stress or pronunciation as well, and learners should use their dictionaries to check if they are not sure.

In each of the last ten exercises, there are two roots, for example **civis** and **colere**. These roots are dealt with together to provide full exercises, and this does not mean that the roots are related, except in the cases of **turba** and **turbo**, and **vacare** and **vanus**. The derivations from each root are listed separately, but they can come up in any order in the exercises themselves.

Pronunciation of Latin words

While it is not essential to pronounce the Latin roots correctly, here are some notes to help anyone wishing to have an approximate pronunciation:

a can be long or short, but may be pronounced /a:/, as in "father", and not like the sound in "name".

e can be long or short, but may be pronounced /e/, as in "met", and not like the sound in "feet".

i can be long or short, but may be pronounced /i/, as in "lit", and not like the sound in "light".

o can be long or short, but may be pronounced /o/, as in "hop", and not like the sound in "hope".

u can be long or short, but may be pronounced /u/, as in "put", and not like the sound in "cut" or in "tune".

au should be pronounced /au/, as in "shout", and not like the sound in "caught".

ae should be pronounced /ai/, as in "light".

c is always pronounced /k/ as in "come", and not like the sound in "cinema", regardless of the vowel which follows.

g is always pronounced /g/ as in "go", and not like the sound in "gentle", regardless of the vowel which follows.

h is always pronounced /h/ as in "home", regardless of its position in the word.

j is always pronounced /j/ as in "yet", and not like the sound in "jet". In classical Latin, **i** was used both as a vowel /i/ and as the consonant /j/.

l is always pronounced /l/ as in "let", and not like the sound in "tell".

ng is always pronounced /ŋg/ as in "finger", and not like the sound in "singer".

qu is always pronounced /kw/ as in "queen".

r should be pronounced as a rolled /r/, but should never be silent as in /ka:/, "car".

s is always pronounced /s/ as in "case", and not like the sound in "cause".

v should be pronounced /w/ as in "wine", but can be pronounced as /v/ as in "vine".

The infinitive verb ending **-re** is always pronounced /re/, rather like "ray", but without the /i/ sound at the end. All the other letters can be pronounced as in Standard English.

Latin prefixes

Many of the derivations in these exercises have prefixes, which usually change their meanings in a predictable way. However, sometimes the original meaning of the prefix is unclear or lost, especially when the meaning of the whole word changes. Some of these are highlighted in the notes below.

Some prefixes can have more than one meaning, and can affect different roots in different ways, but most are included below. Some prefixes also have different forms depending on the first letter of the root word. Such forms are given with examples.

ab-, also **a-**, **abs-**, "from, away, off": *abdicate, ablution, absolve, abstain*

ad-, also **ac-**, **af-**, **ag-**, **al-**, **an-**, **ap-**, **ar-**, **as-**, **at-**, "to, towards, at, up to": *accede, addict, affect, aggravate, alleviate, annotate, appeal, arrest, assimilate, attend*

ambi-/am-, "around, double": *ambidextrous, amputate*

ante-, "before, in front": *antecedent*

bene-, "well": *benefit*

circum-, "round, around": *circumstance*

com-, also **co-**, **col**, **con-**, **cor-**, "with, together, jointly, equally", also used as an intensifier in Latin, and also "totally" in modern English: *coexist, collocate, community, concise, correspond*

contra-, also through French *counter-*, "against": *contradict, counteract*

de-, "down, down from, away from, thoroughly", also "opposite action" in modern English: *decapitate, decrease, defect, degrade, deport*

dis-, also **di-**, **dif-**, also through French *de-*, "apart, separately", also "opposite, lack" in modern English: *disaffected, disclose, disinfect, disjointed, dissolve*

ex-, also **e-**, **ef-**, "out, out of, off, from", also "completely, utterly", and "former, no longer" in modern English: *edict, effect, elevate, exceed, exclude*

extra-, "outside, beyond": *extradite, extraterrestrial*

for- (from **foris**), "outside": *forfeit*

in-, also **il-**, **im-**, **ir-**, also through French *en-*, "in, into, at, on": *enact, enclose, illusion, impulse, include, increase, infect, ingenious*

in-, also **il-**, **im-**, **ir-**, "not", also "opposite, without, absent from" in modern English: *immediate, immunity, incessant, infinity, irregular, irreparable*

inter-, "between, among, within", also "together, with one another" in modern English: *interact, intercede, interlude, intermediate, international*

intra-, **intro-**, "inside, within": *introspection*

mal-, "badly, poorly, abnormally": *malignant*

non-, "not": *nonsense*

ob-, also **oc-**, **of-**, **op-**, "towards, against, in front of, over, away": *obsession, obtain, opportunity, oppressive*

per-, "through, by, during, thoroughly": *perfect, perplex, persist, perspective*

post-, "after": *postgraduate*

prae-, spelled in modern English *pre-*, "before, in front, ahead": *precede, precise, preclude, predict, prefect, pregnant, prepare, president*

pro- also **por-**, **pol-**, also through French *pur-*, "forward, for, instead of, on behalf of", also "in favour of" in modern English: *pollution, proceed, profit, progeny, progress, propel, purport*

re-, also **red-**, "back, backwards, behind", also "again", "in opposition", "repeated" in modern English, or even with no distinct meaning: *react, recede, refine, rejoin, report, repress, resent, resign, resolve, respect, retract*

retro-, "back, backwards": *retrograde, retrospect*

se-, also **sed-**, "apart, apart from, except": *secede, secluded, separate, sever*

sub-, also **suc-**, **suf-**, **sug-**, **sum-**, **sup-**, **sur-**, **sus-**, "under, up from under, upwards, close up to, in substitution, close by", also "further down, lower, slightly" in modern English: *subscribe, subside, subsidy, subsist, succeed, sufficient, support, suppress, resurrect, suspect, sustain*

super-, also through French *sur-*, "above, over, besides, beyond, upon, remaining": *supernatural, supersede, superstition, surfeit, surprise*

trans-, "across, over, beyond, through": *transaction, transgress, transport*

Notes on Latin roots

1. 2. agere *(set in motion, drive, lead, act)*

All the meanings of this root contain the idea of "making things happen", and we can see this in derivations like *act*, *agent* and *agenda*. It also originally had the sense of "drive" and "carry out". Most English words derived from it still carry the ideas of action, movement or making something happen.

3. caedere *(strike, cut, kill)*

In ancient times, killing usually involved cutting, and this root covers both meanings. All the modern derivations are prefixed forms, which change the root **caed/caes** to **cid/cis**. The meaning of "cut" is evident in words like *concise*, originally "cut off, cut short", and *precise*, also originally "cut off, shorten, abridge", while the meaning of "kill" is evident in words like *homicide*, literally "man killing". Only *decide* and *decision* have substantially changed their original meanings from "cut off, terminate" to "put an end to, settle".

4. 5. caput *(head, chief, person)*

Most of the derivations from this root still carry at least an element of the original meaning, and are reflected in the uses of "head" in English. For example, a *chief* is the head person of a group, a *chef* is the head cook in a restaurant and a *cape* is a headland. Less obviously, *capitulate* originally meant "draw up a document in separate headings", and later "surrender under certain terms", and *precipitation* meant "throwing/falling headlong". Even more obscure is *achieve*, from a phrase which originally meant "bring/come to a head" (see Spanish and Portuguese *acabar*, "finish"). However, the original meaning is still recognisable in most derivations.

6. 7. 8. cedere *(go, leave, yield)*

The basic meaning of this root is that of movement, either "go in a certain direction" or "withdraw" and hence, "yield", which is actually the basic meaning of the derivations *cede* and *cease*. Most derivations are prefixed, and the meanings of most of these forms are quite easy to deduce: *accede*, originally "go up to, approach"; *ancestor*, originally **antecessor**, "someone going before"; *concede*, originally "yield completely"; *deceased*, literally "gone away, departed", hence "dead"; *exceed*, literally "go out, go beyond"; *intercede*, literally "go between"; *precede*, literally "go before"; *proceed*, literally "go forward"; *recede*, literally "go back/backwards"; *secede*, literally "go apart"; However, some meanings are not very clearly related to the original meaning: *abscess*, literally "going away", which was used to refer to a medical condition involving fluid congestion; *succeed*, literally "go up to, go near", then "go after, come next" and finally "turn out well".

9. claudere *(bar, close, lock up, conclude)*

Almost all the derivations of this root still remain close to the original meaning: *conclude*, literally "close completely"; *disclose*, literally "unclose, open up"; *enclose* and *include*, literally "close in/inside"; *exclude*, literally "close out"; *preclude*, originally "close ahead of, close off"; *recluse*, originally "shut up/away"; *secluded*, literally "closed apart, shut away from". The original meaning of *clause* was "a section of closed text". The forms spelled like *close* are borrowings from French, while the others come from Latin, whether directly or through French.

10. crescere *(grow, arise, spring)*

Most of the derivations of this root still retain a basic meaning of "grow": *accrete* "literally "grow onto"; *decrease*, literally "grow down"; *increase*, originally "grow in (size)"; *recruit*, literally "grown back". There are two which have significantly changed meanings: *concrete* originally meant "grown together", and hence "become solid", and *crescent* originally referred to the moon as it grew, though it came to describe the shape of the growing moon.

11. dare *(give, offer, pay, allow, put)*

Most of the meanings of the derivations of this root relate to either "give" or "put", though some are not obvious. The meaning of *condone* was originally "grant, permit". A *date* was originally the day a letter was given to someone. *Edit* originally referred to "something produced". *Extradite* was originally "deliver", and a *tradition* was literally a "handing over" from one generation to another. A *mandate* was literally an order to "give by hand". *Render* was altered from the original form **reddere**, literally "give back".

12. 13. dicere *(show, say, speak, specify, mention)*

Most of these derivations are recognisable from their parts: *contradict*, literally "speak against"; *edict*, literally "something spoken out"; *predict*, literally "speak ahead, foretell"; *verdict*, literally "spoken truth". *Diction* originally meant "the way something is said, choice of words", giving rise to *dictionary*, "collection of words".

Some of these derivations are not immediately recognisable as coming from this root. *Condition* originally came from a verb meaning "agree on". *Ditto* is the Italian participle "said". *Addiction* was originally from a verb meaning "declare", which came to mean "devote". *Indict* was originally a verb meaning "inform", and *interdict* was originally "prohibit by speaking". A *ditty* was originally "something dictated", but became a "simple poem or song".

From the extended form **dicare** come: *abdicate*, literally "proclaim away, renounce"; *dedicate*, originally "proclaim, affirm, consecrate"; *indicate*, originally "proclaim" but later "point out, show"; *predicate*, originally "proclaim forth, declare, assert", and *predicament*, originally a "categorisation"; *vindicate*, originally "show authority, assert".

14. duo *(two)*

The original meaning of the root is clearly preserved in all its derivations. The formation **duplus** in Latin, literally "two-fold", gives derivations borrowed directly from Latin like *duplicate*, and others altered in French like *double*.

15. 16. 17. 18. facere *(do, make, create)*

This root is an important contributor of derivations. Most of them still have a basic meaning of "do, make, put", but in many the prefix largely determines the meaning, which is not always clear from the prefix and root combination. While the verb's base root was **fac-**, this changed to **fec-** and **fic-** in compounds: *affect*, literally "do to, act on" and then "strive for, aspire to"; *defect*, originally "do down, desert, fail"; *efficient*, literally "working out, bringing about, accomplishing"; *infect*, literally "do in, put in", hence "taint, spoil"; *perfect*, literally "do completely, accomplish"; *prefect,* literally "make in front, put in front, put in charge"; *proficient*, literally "making forward", hence "progressive"; *suffice*, literally "make up to", hence "supply, be enough".

French also radically changed some forms, like these: *fashion*, originally "making, form", an alternative to *faction*; *affair*, literally "to do"; *feasible*, literally "doable"; *defeat*, another form of *defect*; *counterfeit*, originally "made against", hence "imitated"; *forfeit*, literally "do outside, transgress"; *surfeit*, literally "made over/too much". *Profit* originally meant "make forward, progress, advance". Something which "could be done" in Latin was *facile*, "easy", which also gives the opposite *difficult*. Even Italian supplies *confetti*, along with the French *comfit* and Latin *confection*, all originally referring to things "put together, prepared", in particular "ingredients for making sweets". Originally a *refectory* was a place where monks refreshed themselves. *Manufacture* means literally "make by hand". Finally, the first part of *office* is **opus**, "work", giving the original meaning "doing work".

19. finis *(border, limit, boundary, purpose)*

While most of these derivations still keep much of the original meaning, some are less obvious. The adjective *fine* originally referred to the "limit/height of quality", hence *finery* and *finesse*. From the French *fin*, "end" came *fine*, which originally referred to money which was paid to end a dispute, and also by extension *finance*.

20. frangere *(break, wreck, crush)*

All of these derivations still retain the original meaning of the root. It is interesting to note here how two derivations have different associations and collocations: *fragile*, which retains the original form, is generally applied to things, while *frail*, which was altered in French, is generally applied to people and animals.

21. 22. 23. genus *(kind, tribe)* gignere *(produce, give birth)*
24. nasci *(be born)*

These are three of the most important roots for derivations in modern English vocabulary. They are grouped together because they ultimately share a common Indo-European root, which has the basic meaning of "produce, give birth", and which is also the root of the English words "kin" and "kind". Ironically, the word which actually means "be born", namely **nasci**, is the only one to lose its initial letter, the older form being **gnasci**.

Most of the derivations in English belong to one of the following categories of meaning:
* bearing, birth, determined by birth: *engine, generate, genial, genital, genius, indigenous, ingenious, natal, native, natural, nature, pregnant, progeny*
* of a kind: *gender, general, genre, genus*
* race, clan, nobility: *generous, genteel, gentle, gentry, ingenuous, nation, national*

While most of the words in these exercises have a clear relationship with one of the categories, some are not so obvious. A *genius* was originally a guiding spirit believed to be present at birth, which would act as an inspiration. One's *nature* was originally the character that a person was born with, and this real, natural character was also *genuine*. An inborn quality or skill was originally an *engine*, making the person in question *ingenious*. It might seem that someone born yesterday can be *naïve*, but actually, it is a variant of *native* referring to rustic, uncultured people.

We can classify people and things according to their *gender* and *genre*, or we can just refer to them as *general*. Certain people in ancient societies were different from the rest. They were noble, cultured and freeborn, hence *gentle, genteel, gentry* and *generous*.

25. 26. gradi *(step, walk)* gradus *(step, pace, stage)*

All of the derivations from this root retain the original meanings in one way or another. The idea of movement is clear in derivations: *congress*, literally "walk/come together"; *digress*, literally "step apart"; *ingress* literally "step in"; *progress*, literally "walk forward"; *regression*, literally "walking back"; *transgress*, literally "step across/to the other side". However, some meanings have been extended, as in *aggressive*, formed from a verb which originally meant simply "approach". Similarly,

16

the meaning of "step by step, slowly" is evident in derivations like *gradual* and *gradation*. Almost all the original French forms were replaced by re-borrowed forms from Latin, one survivor being *degree*, originally "rank".

27. gravis *(heavy, serious, weighty, venerable, oppressive)*

The original borrowings from French, including *grief* and *grieve*, carried the main meaning of "oppression" in an emotional sense. Later learned borrowings, directly from Latin or through French, carried the meaning of either "serious" or "heavy", especially with reference to the scientific discoveries of the 17th century relating to *gravity.*

28. jungere *(join, bind, unite)*

As with many other roots, some derivations come directly from French, as with *join* and *joint*, while others are borrowed directly from Latin, as with *junction*. Most of them clearly retain the original meaning: *adjoin*, literally "join to"; *conjoin* and *conjugal*, literally "join together"; *disjointed*, literally "not joined together". However, some meanings have developed away from it: *enjoin*, literally "join on", hence "attach, impose, urge"; *injunction*, originally like *enjoin*, but developing a meaning of "charge, command, order", with specific legal references; *rejoinder*, literally "joining back", but developing a legal meaning of "response to a defendant's plea", before reverting simply to "response".

29. lavare, luere *(wash, moisten, flow over)*

Apart from simply "washing", as in *ablution, launder* and *lavatory,* meanings associated with rivers and rain, give *alluvial* and *deluge*. Other associations with water give *dilute* and *lotion*, while *lavish* extends from the action of pouring rain.

30. levis *(light, nimble, fleeting, trivial, mild)*

Although the basic meaning of the root is "light", many of the derivations come from the verb **levare**, "lighten, raise". The meaning of "light" is evident in *alleviate, levity* and *relief*, from an intensive form literally meaning "lift up, lighten", while "raise" can be seen in *elevate* and *lever*. Extended meanings of both are evident in *leaven, leverage* and *levy,* literally "raising" with special reference to taxes, but far less so in *relevant*, which developed from "lighten" into "connected with, pertaining to".

31. locus *(place, position, situation)*

All of these derivations have clear connections to the original meaning, though *lieu* and *lieutenant* were radically altered by French.

32. ludere *(play, mimic, ridicule, deceive)*

None of the meanings of the derivations has the basic meaning of "play", but they have developed other unpredictable meanings, mostly through the meaning of "mock, ridicule". Here are the original meanings of some of them: *allude*, "refer mockingly"; *collude*, "play together'; *delude*, "play false"; *elude*, "outplay, foil"; *illusion*, "mocking, joking, irony"; *interlude*, "short play between acts in a longer play"; *prelude*, "musical testing before a performance".

33. medius *(middle)*

Most of these derivations carry some or all of the original meaning of being in the middle or in between, including *intermediary*, *mediate*, *medium* and *mean* (altered by French from *median*), while *mediocre* relates to quality rather than position. Less obvious is *immediate*, originally "with nothing in between, direct".

34. memor *(mindful)*

All of these derivations retain the original meaning of the root word in a variety of ways.

35. minus *(less)* minuere *(lessen)*

Most of the derivations retain the idea of "less, lesser", as with *diminish,* literally "make completely small", *minimal* and *minority*. However, a few have moved away from the original meaning in unpredictable directions. Originally a *minister* was someone "inferior" or "subordinate", hence "servant", before developing its modern meanings with its own derivations. *Minute* still keeps its original meaning of "very small" as an adjective, but became applied to time in the phrase **pars minuta prima**, "first small part", to describe the 60th part of an hour.

36. modus *(measure, rhythm, boundary, rule, manner)*

This root gives a wide variety of derivations connected in some way to the idea of measure or manner. Here are the original meanings of some of them: *accommodate*, "make to fit"; *commodity*, "due measure, suitability"; *modest*, "in due measure"; *moderate*, "regulated"; *modify*, "regulate, limit". One derivation from a different meaning of the root is *modern*, originally from **modo**, "by measure, just, just now". The most modern creation is *modem*, a combination of *modulator-demodulator*.

37. munus *(gift, service, office, function)*

All of the derivations have meanings which are extensions of one or other of the original meanings of the root word. All the derivations with the prefix *com-* come from the adjective **communis**, "sharing burdens, sharing duties", and hence "public, common", while *immunity* originally meant "exemption from public duties and charges". *Municipal* originally referred to citizens of self-governing towns, literally "taking office", and *remuneration*, literally "giving back", carries the meaning of "gift, reward".

38. parare *(set, put, prepare)*

In most of these derivations, one of the original meanings is still evident: *apparatus*, "something made ready"; *disparate*, "divided, set apart"; *repair*, "make ready again". The form *pare* was extended from "arrange, adorn" to "trim". Four derivations essentially come from the same form. *Separate*, literally "put apart", was borrowed from Latin, to go along with the earlier French borrowings *sever*, "set apart, separate, cut", *several*, literally "separate, individual", and *severance*, literally "act of separating".

39. 40. pellere *(push, drive, move, thrust)*

This root has two forms, both of which produce derivations: **pell-** and **puls-**. Almost all the derivations carry the original meaning in one way or another, usually defined by the meaning of the prefix: *compel*, originally "drive together", hence "force"; *dispel*, literally "drive apart, away"; *expel*, literally "drive out"; *impel*, literally "drive on"; *propel*, literally "drive forward"; *repel* and *repulse*, literally "drive, push back". Some derivations are less clear. *Pulsate* and *push*, the latter altered through French, are essentially the same verb, denoting a repetitive action of striking or driving. *Pulsar* is a modern astronomical creation from *pulsating star*. *Appeal*, along with its derivation *repeal*, originally meant "drive to court for the payment of debt", becoming "call upon, accuse" in French, and then just "call". It also gives the shortened form *peal*, denoting the ringing of bells.

41. persona *(mask, person)*

All the derivations from this root are clearly associated with the original meaning of "person", so that the meanings of each can be recognised relatively easily. The root word originally referred to the mask worn by an actor, defining a character in a play.

42. placere *(please, satisfy)* placare *(calm, soothe)*

Most of these derivations have been altered by their passage through French, though the original meanings are still in evidence. A few require explanation. *Placebo* was originally the future of the verb "I will please", borrowed to refer to medication which does not necessarily cure the patient but satisfies their desire to be treated. *Plea* originally came from a Latin form of the verb "that which pleases", extending to mean "decree" and then "lawsuit, complaint", and giving rise to the verb *plead*.

43. 44. 45. plicare *(fold, fasten, lay)* plectere *(weave)*

Many of these derivations carry the idea of something being fixed or placed close to something else, while others carry the idea of folding or weaving. A large proportion of these derivations were altered through French, especially those ending in *-ply*. *Apply* and its related derivations carry a basic meaning of "laying something on something else". *Deploy* and *display* were originally the same verb in French, and had the meaning of "unfold". *Employ* originally meant "enfold, involve", as did *imply* and its derivations *implicit* and *implicate*. *Exploit* and *explicit* came from the same verb meaning "unfold", though the former came to mean "something displayed, action, deed", and the latter "explained".

Reply and *replicate* had the same meaning of "fold back, repeat". Something "folded together" can literally be termed *complex*, which also gives *complicate* as well as *complexion*, which originally meant "combination, constitution", then "external expression of constitution", and even *complicity* and *accomplice*, from the idea of "partner, confederate". *Duplicate* meant "fold in two", giving also *duplicity,* originally "ambiguity". French derivations *plait, pleat, pliable* and *pliant*, all involve bending or folding, as does *pliers*. Originally *plight*, with its altered spelling from the original French, meant "folding" and then "condition", before acquiring its negative connotations. Finally, *ply* (as in "ply a trade") is a shortened form of *apply* and shows how far some of these meanings have travelled.

46. 47. porta *(passage, gate, entrance)* portare *(carry, bring)* portus *(harbour, port)*

These roots are ultimately from the same Indo-European root, with the basic meaning of "taking things from one place to another". Most of the derivations have a meaning closely related to the originals, though some have changed. *Disport* and its shortened form *sport*, originally meant "carry away", and then "divert, amuse". While *import* originally meant "bring in, convey", *importance* extended the meaning to "being of consequence, significant". The original meaning of *rapport* came from "bring back", developing into "relationship".

Comport and *portly* both relate to the idea of "bearing". *Purport* moved from the idea of "carry" to "contain", and then "contain a meaning". Finally, there are two words which have completely lost their original associations with the roots: *opportunity* originally had the meaning of a "favourable wind bringing a ship to port", and later the meaning of "fitness, favourable time"; *importune* originally referred to ship without a harbour, hence the meaning of "unfavourable, unfit", developing into the idea of "persistent" and eventually into the verb "ask persistently".

48. potis *(able, capable, possible, strong)*

All the derivations from this root carry one of the original meanings, though *power* has been significantly altered in form by French. *Posse* originally meant "be able/powerful", but was used to denote an armed force of men. *Possess* and other words formed from it actually come from **possidere**, formed from **potis** and **sedere**, literally "sit as master", hence "own, possess".

49. 50. praehendere *(seize, grasp)*

All these derivations have some connection with the original meaning, either physical or mental. However, many have significantly changed in form in their passage through French. Both connections are evident in *apprehend*, literally "seize upon", and its own derivations, but only the mental connection is evident in *comprehend*, literally "seize completely", while *comprehensive* and *comprise* refer to physical attributes. The French borrowings *entrepreneur* and *enterprise* come from the idea of "undertaking, managing", as does the Italian *impresario*.

The idea of "take back" is variously realised in *reprehend, reprieve* and *reprise*, while *surprise* originally meant "overtake", and later "attack unexpectedly, overcome". To *prise* something was originally "grasp, seize", later becoming "lever", while a person who was seized was put in *prison*. Anything seized in battle or any animal caught in a hunt in Roman times was **praeda**, which gives the derivations *predator, predatory* and *prey*.

51. 52. premere *(squeeze, press)*

Almost all these derivations have a recognisable connection with the original meaning. Most of the prefixed forms are recognisable: *compress*, "press together"; *depress*, "press down"; *oppress*, "press against"; *suppress*, "press down/under"; *repress*, "press back". Two derivations have gone their own way. *Express* originally meant "press out", and then "represent, depict, state". With the arrival of trains, an *express* train was one designated as a special service and, by definition, the fastest. *Impress*, "press in, stamp", extended to "make an image" and then "have an effect on". *Print*, borrowed from French, exactly reflects the process of producing the printed page, such that the two words *printing press* essentially mean the same thing. Finally, *reprimand* comes from an alternative form of *repress* with the meaning of "reprove".

53. 54. pungere *(prick, pierce, sting)*

Most of these derivations are recognisably from the original root, but some have moved a long way. Derivations like *point, punctual, puncture* and *punctuation* still carry meanings related to the form or action of a point in time or place, as well as to piercing, though *point* has developed other meanings like "moment, chance, subject". Other derivations have changed: *pungent*, literally "piercing", now usually refers to strong smells; the French form *poignant*, also literally "piercing", now only denotes mental or emotional distress; *punch* originally only referred to a "pointed tool", but extended to "strike with a fist"; the alternative form *pounce* also originally referred to a "pointed tool", but extended to mean a "bird's talon", and then extended further to mean the action of seizing with talons or claws; *punctilious* comes from an Italian word meaning "fine point, trivial objection", with the idea of being very careful or exact.

There are also some prefixed forms: *appoint,* originally "come to a point, agree", and then "put in office", and its opposite, *disappoint*, literally "to remove from office", extending to "frustrate expectations"; *compunction*, literally "thorough pricking" with reference to the conscience, hence "regret, remorse"; *expunge*, literally "prick out", a process by which list items were marked out with a prick for removal.

55. 56. 57. regere *(rule, direct, guide)*

This Latin root is ultimately related to the English "right", and basically carries the meanings of "straighten, correct, regulate, guide". The meanings that extend from these include ideas both of keeping or making things straight or right, and of ruling or controlling, in which we can see the connection with **rex**, "ruler, king".

The connection with the meaning "king" can be seen in derivations like *regal* and the French forms *royal* and *realm*, and the connected meaning of "rule, ruling" is evident in *reign, regime, regimen* and *regiment.* The idea of keeping things straight and under control can be seen in derivations like *rule, regulate* and *rectify,* while a *rail* physically keeps things straight or in order. In Roman times an area of land under a particular direction or rule was a *region.*

Some of the prefixed derivations have moved a long way from the original form and meaning. To *correct* was to "make completely straight". To *direct* was to "set straight", which also gives us forms radically altered by French, including *dress*, "direct, guide, arrange", *address*, "direct towards" and *adroit*, "right, just". To *erect* was to "set out, set up". One other form, contracted from **subregere**, "go straight up, rise", is *surge,* which also gives derivations like *resurrect* and *insurgent.*

58. sacer *(sacred, holy)* sancire *(make sacred, confirm)*

Most of these derivations are easily recognisable. Two might require explanation. *Execrable* comes from a verb meaning "curse", while *sanction* carries the meaning "decree, ordinance" rather than any meaning related to holiness.

59. 60. sedere *(sit, linger, remain, settle)*

Many of these derivations recognisably involve sitting or remaining, including *preside*, "sit before, in front", *reside* and *residue*, "remain behind", *sedate*, "settled, calm", *sedentary*, "sitting", *sediment*, "settling", *session*, "act of sitting", and *séance*, "sitting". From the French for "seat" comes *siege*, which referred the act of an army sitting round a town. Someone who is literally "sitting apart" is a *dissident.*

Other derivations have less recognisable connections with the original root. A person who would "sit beside another", usually a judge, had to *assess* others, mainly for tax. This derivation also gives *assize* and *size*, originally "assessment, regulation", and then "amount, extent". Another derivation from the same form is *assiduous*, literally "sitting close up, occupied, unremitting". Someone who would "settle on, occupy" a position might also be lying in wait to ambush another, hence *insidious.* Anyone "sitting behind, near" would be there ready to assist, hence *subsidy* and *subsidiary.* From the same form, *subside* took a different route as "sit down, settle down". *Supersede* originally meant "sit above, stay clear of", and then "delay, defer", before taking its modern meaning. Finally, something which might "sit opposite" could "occupy, besiege" a person in such a way as to become an *obsession.*

61. 62. sentire *(perceive, feel)*

Most of the meanings of the derivations of this root relate to either the head or the heart. For example, *sense, sensible, assent* and *consensus* have mental connotations, while *sensitive, sensual* and *sentimental* have emotional connotations. Other derivations relate to perception or detection, for example *sensory, sentient* and *sensor.* Some connections are less obvious. *Sentence* originally meant "judgement, opinion, thought", but then developed legal and grammatical connotations. *Sense* carries ideas related to more than one area of meaning.

63. signum *(mark, sign, token, image)*

Most of the derivations of this root have either physical connotations, for example *signal*, or abstract connotations, for example *signify*, and a few, such as *sign,* have both. *Seal*, which was radically altered in French from the Latin **sigillum**, originally meant "design", and came to refer to the wax stamp closing a document. Certain verbs have moved away from the original meaning: *assign*, originally "mark out"; *consign*, originally "mark with a seal" and then "ratify, attest"; *design*, originally "mark out"; *resign*, originally "check off" in connection with making entries in an accounts book, and later "cancel, give up".

64. similis *(like, similar)*

This root, and the roots in the next section, are all related to the English word "same" in form and meaning. All the derivations retain meanings closely related to the original meaning, although in *dissemble* the meaning stretches to "pretend" and "disguise".

65. singulus *(single)* simplex *(single, simple)* simul *(together)*

All these roots are related to **similis** in the previous section. Derivations have clear connections: **singulus** - *single, singular*; **simplex** - *simple, simpleton, simplify, simply, simplicity, simplistic*; **simul** - *assemble, assembly, disassemble, ensemble*.

66. solvere *(loosen, dissolve)*

Technically, this root is itself a compound **seluere**, "wash away", which is derived from **lavare/luere**, "wash". The main meanings in Latin were "loosen, dissolve, break up", which are clearly visible in derivations like *absolve*, literally "loosen from, free from", *dissolve*, literally "loosen apart", *soluble*, *solvent* and *solution*. The modern meanings of "find answers" and "decide" in *solve, resolve, resolute* and *resolution* developed after the words were borrowed into English. Lastly, the original meaning of *absolute* was "set free, made separate, complete", which later changed to "perfect, free from defect".

67. 68. 69. 70. specere *(look)*

The vast majority of the modern derivations from this root still have a clear connection with the basic meaning of "look", or with the related meanings of "observe, examine, consider". *Spectre* was originally "something looked at, apparition", though *spectrum* is a modern borrowing. One important word from this root is *species*, originally "appearance, form", and later "kind, sort", as it gives a number of further derivations including *special*, originally "of a kind", *specific* and other forms associated with them.

Some of the prefixed forms retain the original meaning more than others. *Aspect* originally meant simply "look, appearance", but when it was borrowed, it referred to the appearance of planets, before it took on its modern meanings. *Conspicuous* comes from a verb with the original meaning of "see completely" and "catch sight of, notice". The original literal meaning of *despise, despicable, despite* and its shortened form *spite* was "look down on", extending to "scorn". Similarly, the original, literal meaning of *expect* was "look out", extending to "wait and see, hope". *Inspection* originally meant "look into" and by extension "examine", and *introspection* meant literally "look inward".

Perspicacious comes from a verb originally meaning "look through, look at closely", as does *perspective*, though its modern meanings developed after it was borrowed. *Prospect* and its related forms come from a verb meaning "look forward, look out on", and developed further meanings after coming into English. *Respect* comes from a verb meaning "look back, regard, consider", extending to "regard highly", with another extension to "delay", which is also the original meaning of *respite*. Another verb meaning "look back" gives *retrospect*. *Suspect* comes from a verb with the original meaning of "look up at", with the extended meaning of "look askance", hence "mistrust".

71. 72. 73. 74. 75. stare *(stand)*

This root gives English a huge variety of derivations, most of which still retain a connection, however tenuous, with the original meaning of "stand" or with one of the extended meanings like "stay, stand firm, be in a position, be fixed". There are two extended forms in Latin which give further derivations: **sistere**, "make stand, cause to stand", and **statuere** (also in the combining form **–stituere**), "enact, establish, fix, decide".

The original meanings can be seen in derivations like *stable,* literally "able to stand, firm", *stage,* ultimately from Latin **staticum**, "a place to stand", *stance*, "standing place, position", and *stay.* A *state* was originally a "manner of standing, position", and was used in Roman times to refer to the state of the republic, i.e. "government". It was later used as a verb in English meaning "place", and then "put in words", hence *statement.* Two evidently French forms are *estate*, which originally meant the same as *state*, but came to refer to property, and *establish*, literally "make stable". Other interesting derivations are *stationary,* which originally referred to a military station, *statistics*, which originally referred to the academic teaching of *state* (as in government) affairs*,* and *staunch*, which originally referred to rivers stopping and drying up, then took the meaning "watertight", and from that "firm, intact", in a sense coming full circle.

There are many prefixed forms, including the following: *rest*, literally "stand one's ground, remain behind", giving "what is left over, what remains" (totally unconnected with "rest" meaning "repose, relax"); the further prefixed form *arrest*, meaning "stop, restrain"; *circumstance*, literally "standing round"; *constant*, literally "standing firm, immovable"; *contrast*, literally "contend, stand out against"; *distance*, literally "standing apart"; *extant*, literally "standing out, visible"; *instant*, literally "standing on, pressing on, urgent" with particular reference to time; *obstacle*, literally "something standing opposite, hindering"; *substance*, literally "what stands under", or "the underlying essence" of something. From a related root **stanare** come *destine*, which meant "make firm, appoint, determine", and *obstinate*, which meant "persistent, resolute, stubborn". Finally, from an old form **superstes**, "standing over, above", often as a witness or in triumph, we get *superstition*, which meant in Roman times "excessive fear of the gods".

From **sistere** comes a group of prefixed forms which mostly share an idea of "being firm/resolute" and "not changing": *assist*, literally "stand by, near", with special reference to legal defence; *consist*, an intensive form meaning "take a standing position, remain firm"; *desist*, literally "come to a standstill"; *exist*, literally "step out, stand forward, arise"; *insist*, literally "stand on, stand one's ground, remain"; *persist*, literally "take a continuous stand"; *resist*, literally "halt, stand against, withstand"; and finally, *subsist*, literally "stand up, withstand, support, continue".

From **statuere** and its combining form **–stituere** comes another group of forms which generally share an idea of "being fixed", including these: *statue* and *statute*, literally "something enacted, put in place, established"; *constitute*, literally "set up, establish"; *destitute*, literally "put away, set apart, abandoned"; *institute*, literally "set in place, fix, establish"; *prostitution*, literally "offering for sale", from Roman times usually, referring to offering women for sex; *restitution*, literally "putting back in place, restoring"; and finally *substitute*, something "placed under, next to" or "put in place of" something else.

76. tempus *(time, season)*

The basic meaning of "time" only really comes through in *contemporary*, *tempo*, *temporary*, *tense* and *temporal*, although even the meaning of *temporal* has been extended to "secular". In *extemporise* the idea of "time" is extended to doing something "according to the needs of the moment", hence "improvise". The other derivations take their meaning from the idea of "proper time", "right season" or "good measure". The verb *temper* meant "regulate, measure, combine, moderate", from which we get the noun *temper*, originally "balance, proportion". The meanings of *temperance*, *temperament*, *temperate* and *temperature* all come from the idea of "moderation".

77. 78. 79. tendere *(stretch, aim, strive)*

Most of the derivations from this root still carry one of the original meanings. The meaning of "stretch" is evident in *tense, tensile* and *tension*, while a *tent* was originally made of animal skins stretched over poles. Similarly, *extend, extension* and *extensive* all carry the idea of "stretching out"; and *intense, intensity, intensive* and *intensify* carry the idea of "stretching towards, straining". Another extension of "stretch" is seen in *attend, attentive* and *attention*, literally "stretch to", but with particular application to the mind, hence "listen". The meaning of "swollen" is evident in *distended* while the meaning of "slackening" is evident in *détente*.

The meaning of "aim" can be seen in *intend, intent* and *intention*, stretching to "understanding" in *entente*. The original meaning of *tend* and *tendency* was "incline", while *tendentious* takes the meaning further into "inclining towards a particular side". The meaning of "strive" is seen most clearly in the intensive forms *contend, contention* and *contentious*.

26

Three other types of derivation have moved away from the original meaning. Originally *ostensibly* and *ostentatious* carried the idea of "stretch towards" which developed into "show"; similarly, the original idea behind *pretend, pretence* and *pretentious* was "stretch towards/in front", which in turn developed into "hold out, present", and eventually "allege, claim (falsely)"; finally, also with the original meaning of "stretch forward", *portend* and *portent* came to refer to the future, as in "foretell, presage, warn".

80. 81. 82. tenere *(hold, keep)*

Most of these derivations still carry much of the original meanings of "hold, keep", as we can see in the following: *tenable, tenacious, tenant* (literally "someone holding"), *tenement* (literally a "holding")*, tenet* (literally "he/she holds") and *tenure*, although *tenor*, originally "holding on", took the meaning of "contents" and then "substance".

The original meanings of the prefixed forms are generally easily recognisable: *abstain*, literally "hold away, withhold"; *contain* and *content,* literally "hold together, restrain, hold inside", though *content* and *contentment* extended to "self-contained, satisfied"; *continue*, also literally "hold together", but in the sense of "join, connect" in an uninterrupted way, which also gives *continent*, "continuous, uninterrupted (land mass)"; *countenance,* literally "holding together, self-control", which extended to "bearing, behaviour, expression, appearance".

Other prefixed forms are these: *detain*, literally "hold off, keep back"; *entertain*, literally "hold together, support, maintain" and later "show hospitality"; *lieutenant*, literally "placeholder"; *maintain*, literally "hold in the hand, keep hold of" and then "keep up, support"; *obtain*, literally "hold to, get, acquire"; *pertain*, literally "stretch out to, relate to"; *retain*, literally "hold back", and from the extended meaning "employ", the form *retinue*, "people employed, group of followers"; finally, *sustain*, literally "hold up, support".

83. terminus *(end, limit, boundary)*

Most derivations of this root still have the original meaning denoting a boundary or limit, either in time or space. The original meaning of *determine* was literally "mark off a boundary, delimit", and later became "decide, interpret". One fundamental shift in meaning is evident in *term* and *terminology*, with the meaning of "word, expression", which resulted from the use of **terminus** in Late Latin to denote an element of a mathematical ratio or logical expression.

84. terra *(ground, earth, land)*

All of these derivations still carry the original meaning, either in the sense of "land" or "planet Earth", for example *inter*, literally "put in earth", *terracotta*, literally "baked earth" and *extraterrestrial*, literally "outside the Earth".

85. 86. 87. trahere *(draw, trail, pull)*

Some of the meanings of these derivations have moved away from the original meanings, but the modern meanings can be traced back. The original meaning of this root, "draw, pull" was extended in other forms to mean "manage, handle". *Traction*, literally "pulling", and *tractor*, literally "puller", both retain the meaning. *Trail* and *train* carry the basic meaning of "pull behind, drag". *Treat, treatise, treatment, treaty* and *tractable* all retain the basic meaning of "handle, manage". *Trace, tract* and *trait* all carry the basic meaning of "mark out, delineate".

The prefixed forms also largely retain elements of the original meanings: *abstract,* literally "draw away", later developing the different ideas of "not concrete" and "summary"; *attract,* literally "pull towards"; *contract,* literally "pull together", later extending to both "combine, make an agreement" and "make narrow"; *detract,* literally "pull down, disparage"; *distract* and *distraught,* literally "pull away/apart, unsettle"; *extract,* literally "draw out"; *portray,* literally "draw forward, trace a line, paint"; similarly, *protracted,* literally "drawn forward/out, lengthened (in time); *retract* and *retreat* both literally "draw back"; and finally *subtract,* literally "draw from under, draw off, take away".

88. vivere *(live)*

Most of these derivations still retain the basic meanings of "live, life": *vitamin, revitalise, revive* and *survive.* Some relate to life in the sense of "liveliness", e.g. *vitality, vivacious, convivial* and *vivid. Viable* has the sense of "able to live", while *vital* has the sense of "necessary for life".

89. 90. vocare *(call, summon)* vox *(voice, sound, call, language)*

The majority of these derivations, such as *voice, vocal, vocalise, vocalist* and *vociferous,* still retain a strong element of the original meanings, though some are less evidently connected, for example *vocation,* literally "a calling" (in a spiritual or religious sense), and later "occupation, profession". Originally, *vocabulary* was a "list of words", from **vocabulum**, "name, noun, word". *Vowel* comes through French from **litera vocalis**, literally "vocal letter". Also through French comes *vouch,* originally "summon to court to prove a title", hence "invoke, claim, guarantee", along with the noun *voucher,* "summoning" and later "guarantee, receipt". Originally *equivocal* meant "of identical sound", becoming later "ambiguous, vague".

The prefixed forms also retain much of the original meanings: *advocate,* literally "call to, call as a witness"; *convocation,* literally "calling together"; *evoke,* literally "call out"; *invoke,* literally "call upon summon, appeal to"; *provoke,* literally "call forth, challenge, excite"; and *revoke,* literally "call back, rescind, repeal".

91. civis *(resident, citizen)*; colere *(tend, worship)*

The derivations from **civis** contain ideas associated with life in a *city*, whether in connection with activity in the city itself, as with *civic*, or in connection with the type of society associated with city (as opposed to country) life, as in *civil*, *civility* and by extension *civilisation*. The derivations from **colere** generally relate to the idea of "tend, educate", as in *cultivate*, either in relation to the land or the mind, hence *culture*. The meaning of *colony* comes from the idea of a place which is settled and cultivated.

92. damnum *(loss, penalty)*; durus *(long-lasting, rough, hard)*

All of the derivations from **damnum** still carry ideas of "loss, penalty, blame, punishment". The derivations of **durus** carry the original meanings of either "rough, hard" as in *dour*, *duress* and *obdurate*, or "last long", as in *durable*, *duration*, *during* and *endure*.

93. fallere *(do wrong, deceive, cheat)*; fendere *(strike, push)*

All the derivations of **fallere** carry the idea of "mistake, do wrongly" as in *default*, *fallible*, *fail* and *fault*, or of "deceive, cheat" as in *fallacy*, *false* and *falsify*. All the derivations of **fendere** carry the original meaning of "strike", either to protect as in *defend*, *defence*, *fend*, or to attack as in *offence*, *offend*.

94. labor *(toil, effort, work)*; liber *(free)*

The derivations from **labor** are clearly related to work, often hard work, in one way or another: *elaborate*, literally "work out"; *collaborate*, literally "work together"; *labour*, *laboratory* and *laborious*. Most of the derivations from **liber** have the meaning of "freedom" at their heart, including *illiberal*, *liberal*, *liberate*, *liberty* and *libertarian*. Originally, *libertine* meant "freedman" before it developed into "dissolute person", and *deliver* originally meant "free from, set free".

95. mirus *(wonderful, astonishing)*; mutare *(shift, change)*

All the derivations from **mirus** carry the meaning of either "wonder", as in *marvellous*, *miracle* and *miraculous*, or "look" from the idea of "look in wonder", as in *admire*, *mirage* and *mirror*. Most of the derivations from **mutare** still carry the meaning of "change", as with *mutant*, *mutate* and *permutation*, though *mutual* carries the idea of "exchange". Originally *commute* also carried the idea of "exchange, interchange", though it took the meaning of "travel to and from work regularly" from the idea of buying a *commutation* (season) ticket for travel, hence *commuter*.

96. pretium (reward, value); proprius (peculiar, personal)

The derivations of **pretium** carry the meaning of either "value" in some way, as in *appraise, appreciate, appreciative, price, precious* and *praise,* or "reward", as in *prize.* With **proprius** the idea of "personal, one's own" is evident in *expropriate, property* and *proprietor.* The idea of "peculiar, special" and by extension "correct" is present in *appropriate* and *proper.*

97. sanus (healthy); satis (enough)

The derivations from **sanus** carry a meaning denoting either physical health, as in *unsanitary, sanatorium, sanitation* and *sanitise,* or mental health, as in *sane* and *sanity.* With **satis** the idea of "enough" is clear in *dissatisfied, satiate, satisfaction, satisfy* and *saturate,* while the meaning of *asset* comes from an old legal term in Anglo-French, *aver assetz,* literally "to have enough" to meet a legal claim.

98. scire (know); spondere (pledge, promise)

The idea of "know, be aware" is present in the derivations from **scire**, like *conscience, conscientious, conscious, unconscious* and *science.* The original idea of "pledge, promise" is clear in the derivations from **spondere** like *sponsor* and *spouse,* literally "someone promised, betrothed, bride/groom". Originally, *respond* meant "promise back/in return", hence "answer, reply"; the further extended form *correspond* meant originally "be in harmony, agree", and later "exchange communications". Originally **despondere** in Latin described a reversal of a marriage betrothal, but came to mean just "lose heart, resign", hence *despondent.* The modern meanings of *responsible* developed relatively recently.

99. torquere (twist, turn, wind); turba (disorder, riot, mob); turbo (eddy)

Most of the derivations from **torquere** still carry some of the original meaning, particularly into the extended meanings of "pain, suffering". The derivation with the closest meaning to the original is *tortuous; contort* denotes an intensive type of twisting; similarly *distort* originally meant "twist completely, twist different ways"; *extort* literally meant "twist out, wrest away", before becoming "obtain money with threats". Finally *torment* and *torture* show how "twisting" can be applied to people to cause extreme pain and suffering.

All of the derivations from **turba** retain the original meanings of restlessness or agitation, as can be seen in *trouble* and *turbulent; disturb* originally meant "disorder completely" and later "stir up, agitate", while *perturb* had similar origins. "Stirring up" mud makes water *turbid.* Finally, from **turbo** comes *turbine,* which retains the original circular, twisting motion.

100. vacare (*be empty*) vanus (*empty*)

These roots are related to each other, as their derivations clearly demonstrate, most clearly in *vacate, vacant, vacuous, vacuum* and *evacuate*. From an altered Latin root form, further altered in French, come *void* and the further derivations *avoid* and *avoidance*, originally "empty out", and *devoid*, originally "empty away, remove, vacate". *Vanish* moved from the idea of "be empty" to "disappear", while *vain* developed the idea of "worthless" and later, along with *vanity*, the meanings of "proud, conceited".

1. agere 1

Put the most suitable word in each space. Think about the part of speech required in each space. Make sure you use the correct form.

act (n), acting (adj), active, actor, actual, agency, agenda, agent, agile, agitate, navigate, reaction

1. The narrow channels and small islands on this part of the coast are very difficult to _____. You need a ship's pilot who knows the area.

2. These monkeys are extremely light and _____. They can run up and down trees and swing through them quickly and easily.

3. If you want to be a writer, you need to have an _____ who knows the business and who can talk to publishers for you and offer them your work.

4. When I told Jan she had passed all her exams, she just looked blankly at me and carried on watching TV. It wasn't the _____ I had expected.

5. The dog had been sleeping quietly, but suddenly jumped up and became extremely _____. Then I realised that he had felt the earthquake before it hit.

6. OK everyone. Let's get the meeting started so we can finish on time. The first item on the _____ is the move to the new building next month.

7. My new car is in such good condition that all my friends thought that I had paid at least £10,000 for it. The _____ price was only £5000.

8. Nowadays it's much cheaper and less complicated for the college to hire a temporary teacher from an _____ than to employ one directly.

9. When Sam saw the little girl screaming for help at the window of the burning house, he ran in and brought her out. It was a really brave _____.

10. While Mr Jones is recovering from his operation, I'll be the _____ head teacher. Until he returns I'll try to perform as well as he has.

11. While the President may well be involved in this political scandal in some way, the principal _____ in this affair is the President's Chief of Staff.

12. Nowadays more and more people live longer, remain in good health and stay _____ into their old age, even taking up new sports.

2. agere 2

Put the most suitable word in each space. Think about the part of speech required in each space. Make sure you use the correct form.

act (v), acting (n), action, actionable, activate, counteract, enact, exacting, interact, proactive, react, transaction

1. Don't forget to press the red button by the door before leaving the house. It will _____ the security system ten seconds after you close the door.
2. If you feel sick on the journey, take these pills. They'll _____ the effects of the travel sickness and you'll quickly feel a lot better.
3. I saw that new science fiction film "Star Sailors" last night. The camerawork and special effects were really good but the _____ was really awful.
4. After I finish putting your details into the computer, your new savings account will become _____ and you can start using it straight away.
5. The government intends to _____ a new law to create more jobs and bring more unemployed people back into the workforce.
6. The problem with the management in this company is that there's too much talk and not enough _____. The managers need to do something soon.
7. I think someone has been using my credit card. There's a _____ for a new television on my statement, but I don't remember making it.
8. Remember that our opponents in this game are a very hard team. If one of their players kicks you, it's vitally important that you don't _____.
9. I thought that I was really fit and healthy, but I found this army training course far more _____ than I thought. I'm exhausted! I need a good rest.
10. This is a commercial opportunity that won't last forever, so you need to _____ now and take it if you want to make the best of it.
11. The great thing about travelling around other countries is that you meet a lot of people that you can _____ with and really get to know.
12. Your problem is that you always wait for work opportunities to come your way. You should be far more _____ and create your own opportunities.

3. caedere

Put the most suitable word in each space. Think about the part of speech required in each space. Make sure you use the correct form.

concise, decide, decisive, excise, fratricide, homicide, incision, incisive, précis, precise, precision, suicide

1. Jim's comments in the debate were so _____ and persuasive that he completely destroyed the other team's arguments and his team won easily.
2. In the past when a king died, his sons would often compete to succeed him as king. This often led to _____, when one brother killed the others.
3. I can't tell you the _____ amount you will get from the return on your investment until we complete the process, but it should be about £100,000.
4. In this reading test, the important information is usually contained in only one or two words, so make your answers as _____ as possible.
5. The operation was a success as the surgeons managed to _____ the whole of the brain tumour, so we hope your husband makes a full recovery.
6. Both universities have made me a good offer of a place for next year, but I simply can't _____ which is better. Which one should I choose?
7. When the police found the gun in the dead man's hand they thought it was _____, but there's new evidence that he didn't actually kill himself.
8. The whole annual report is about 20,000 words, so I have to read through it and then write a _____ of it in about 1000 words for the next meeting.
9. William's victory at Hastings in 1066 was a _____ event in English language history, because it meant French would become the dominant language.
10. At the start of the operation, the surgeon picked up his scalpel and carefully made a deep _____ in the patient's chest.
11. I'm afraid this microscope isn't good enough to examine micro-organisms. We need one with far greater _____ and detail.
12. When the police entered the house they found three dead bodies, so they called in detectives from the _____ division to investigate.

4. caput 1

Put the most suitable word in each space. Think about the part of speech required in each space. Make sure you use the correct form.

achieve, cape, capital (2), capitation, cattle, chapter, chef, chief, recapitulate

1. This book is so exciting I can't put it down. I started it this morning and I've almost reached the final _____.
2. Some farms in Australia are so big that they have thousands of _____ which roam over huge areas of open country.
3. The sea was quite rough, but after we sailed round the _____ we found a sheltered harbour to anchor the boat for the night.
4. The first _____ of Roman Britain was Colchester, but it was later moved to London, which had become the biggest city.
5. There are many reasons why this business plan failed, but the _____ reason is that we simply didn't have enough money to make it work.
6. Right, so just to make sure everyone understands what we have to do, I'm going to _____. If you're still not sure, please tell me.
7. The tennis player, Roger Hinton, has announced his retirement. During his career the highest position he _____ in the world rankings was number three.
8. We've decided to go on strike for more money, so everyone has to pay a _____ fee in order to support our action against the management.
9. After three years in France studying haute cuisine, Paul Taylor became a _____ at one of the best restaurants in London.
10. If we're going to set up this company properly we need to raise a lot more _____. We could ask the bank for a loan or get people to invest.

5. caput 2

Put the most suitable word in each space. Think about the part of speech required in each space. Make sure you use the correct form.

cape, capital, capitalise, capitulate, captain, chieftain, decapitate, precipice, precipitation, precipitous

1. The north coast of the island has gentle slopes and long beaches, but the south coast is lined with _____ cliffs, which drop straight into the sea.

2. The manager tried desperately to keep his job, but when he realised he had lost the trust of the players, he finally _____ and announced he was leaving.

3. When I was a girl, I had a big waterproof _____, which I would put on to cover my clothes whenever I went out in the rain.

4. Good morning. This is your _____ speaking. We will be flying at an altitude of ten thousand metres and the flight time to New York is four hours.

5. A good chess player should _____ on the mistakes that an opponent makes. You have to be ruthless and single-minded if you want to win.

6. The road through the mountains was so narrow and dangerous that we were very lucky not to go over a _____ and down into the river far below.

7. In ancient times, it was customary every summer for the _____ of all the tribes in the area to come together and settle disputes over a great feast.

8. The British government finally abolished _____ punishment in 1965. Since then, the sentence for murder has been life imprisonment.

9. The guillotine was used in the French Revolution to _____ enemies of the state as quickly as possible.

10. This area has such a low level of annual _____ that most of it is desert and it is very difficult to grow crops without irrigation.

6. cedere 1

Put the most suitable word in each space. Think about the part of speech required in each space. Make sure you use the correct form.

abscess, cede, concede, concession, precede, predecessor, succeed, success, successful, succession, successive, successor

1. A volcanic eruption is often _____ by a series of earthquakes, which can act as a warning for people to leave the area before the eruption.

2. After the First World War, Germany was forced to _____ territory to some of the countries bordering it, including France and Poland.

3. I'd like to thank you all for your hard work in making this year's festival the most _____ one we have had since the society started. It went so well.

4. Terry had to go to hospital to have an operation on a bad _____ in his leg, which was becoming very swollen and painful.

5. After the election, the outgoing President told reporters today that he wished his _____ all the best in his new post.

6. The two sides in the pay dispute finally came to an agreement after each made significant _____ in their demands to the other side.

7. After ten _____ wins, our team is now playing great football and has got to the top of the league table. Today should be the eleventh win in a row.

8. I _____ that you didn't have all the help and time you needed to complete your project, but you still should have tried harder to get a better result.

9. If you want to _____ in your studies and go to university, you really have to study harder and complete all your work on time.

10. The new manager thanked his _____ for all the hard work he had done, and expressed his desire to maintain his high standards.

11. John lost his job because he was late to work three days in _____ and the manager just lost his patience.

12. As you all know, Sally is leaving today for a new managerial post after ten years here. We would all like to wish her every _____ in her new job.

7. cedere 2

Put the most suitable word in each space. Think about the part of speech required in each space. Make sure you use the correct form.

accede, access, accession, accessory, procedure, proceed, process, procession, recede, recess, recession, secede

1. The Prime Minister today stated that the economy was not heading for a _____, but would continue to grow, although much more slowly.

2. This beautiful two-piece outfit comes with many matching _____, including gloves, a hat and a scarf.

3. You have to follow the correct _____ for buying new equipment. Fill in the order form, get the manager to sign it and then send it to accounts.

4. On the morning of the wedding, the bride, groom and their families and guests go in a big _____ along the road from the house to the church.

5. After five days of heavy rain and flooding, the water has finally started to _____, gradually revealing damaged houses and dead animals.

6. The company is going to invest in new machinery, which will greatly speed up the manufacturing _____ and increase production and profits.

7. The day before his _____ to the post of chief executive of the company, Mr Stevens decided the job was not for him and didn't take it up.

8. After they had arrested the suspects and brought to the police station, detectives _____ to question them about the explosions the week before.

9. At the back of the Roman villa there was a small _____ in the wall, where the archaeological team found a jar containing a hundred gold coins.

10. The people of the southern region voted to _____ from the country, so the government sent in the army. That's how the fighting started.

11. The library has installed a ramp at the entrance to allow people in wheelchairs to _____ the building more easily.

12. The strike finally ended after three days of tough negotiations, when the management finally _____ to the workers' demands for more pay.

8. cedere 3

Put the most suitable word in each space. Think about the part of speech required in each space. Make sure you use the correct form.

ancestor, ancestry, cease, cessation, deceased, exceed, excess, excessive, incessant, intercede, precedent, predecease

1. It's no good. I can't bear the _____ noise from the road works. It's been going on all day. I wish they'd stop for a few minutes so I can think.

2. Maria is a typically English woman, although her _____ all came from Italy a hundred years ago to find work in London.

3. After six hours the snowstorm finally _____ and the sky cleared. Everything was covered in deep, crisp snow, gleaming in the evening sun.

4. Harry saw two people arguing furiously in the street yesterday. When he tried to _____ and calm them down, they told him to shut up and go away.

5. It's fantastic! The exam results of the whole class _____ all our expectations. Everyone passed with at least a C grade, even lazy Larry.

6. Tom spent twenty years looking for his real parents. When he finally found his mother, she told him that his father was already sadly _____.

7. The most interesting thing about this judgement from the court is that there was no _____ from history to follow. This is the first time it's happened.

8. Tony was the last person in his family to die. His parents and brothers and sisters all _____ him.

9. I recently found out that I have a long and noble _____, dating back three hundred years to the king's brother, so you should treat me with due respect!

10. The two warring countries agreed to a _____ of hostilities and the start of negotiations with a UN representative to resolve the border dispute.

11. Although the suspect had tried to resist arrest, he accused the police of using _____ force to control him, resulting in him breaking two ribs.

12. These days, if your luggage is over the normal weight limit, airlines charge a lot of money to carry your _____ baggage.

9. claudere

Put the most suitable word in each space. Think about the part of speech required in each space. Make sure you use the correct form.

clause, close, closet, closure, conclude, disclose, enclose, exclude, include, preclude, recluse, secluded

1. The _____ of the car factory severely affected the local working population and left many people without work, or even the possibility of work.

2. The journalist refused to _____ the source of his information on the terrorist organisation, so the judge sent him to prison for 6 months.

3. We spent our holiday in a lovely cottage in a _____ valley in the mountains of Scotland. We hardly saw anybody else the whole time.

4. There's a _____ in the loan contract which says the bank can take possession of your house if you miss a monthly payment.

5. The party conference _____ with a rousing speech by the leader, which received a standing ovation. Everyone went home happy.

6. Nobody knew that Keith was a _____ gambler until his wife found out that their bank account was empty and all their savings had gone.

7. Old Seth is a _____ who lives in a dirty old hut in the woods outside the town. He generally avoids people and doesn't like visitors.

8. There was a very _____ finish to the men's 100 metres at the Olympics, with Roy Laporta winning the gold by 2/100s of a second.

9. For added security, the house and grounds are _____ by a high wall, with CCTV cameras and searchlights to keep away unwelcome visitors.

10. You should check your house carefully and make sure it's secure before you go on holiday, to _____ any possibility of someone breaking in.

11. Nathaniel! Can you listen? This activity _____ you, so you need to pay attention or you won't know what to do.

12. The total cost of this home cinema system is £1000, _____ sales tax, which comes to an extra £150, making a total of £1150.

10. crescere

Put the most suitable word in each space. Think about the part of speech required in each space. Make sure you use the correct form.

accrete, accrue, concrete, crescendo, crescent, decrease, decrement, increase, increment, recruit

1. This shape is called a _____ because it is shaped like the waxing moon in its first quarter.

2. You should leave your savings in the bank to _____ over the next few years so that you can use the money to finance your studies in the future.

3. The trial period for this computer programme is set to _____ every day till it reaches the end. The software cannot be used again unless you buy a licence.

4. At the meeting last night we came up with a _____ solution to the loss in sales. We're going to increase the advertising budget and plan a new campaign.

5. We are a growing company and we have to _____ new workers to staff the offices that we're going to open in Paris and New York.

6. In the final movement, the symphony rises to a huge _____, and then quickly dies away, ending on a simple, sad note.

7. The government today decided to cut interest rates after the inflation figures showed a sharp _____, down to 2.5%.

8. Every year you are at this company, you will get a 5% _____ in your salary till you reach the top of the salary scale in about six years.

9. Ten years after the cruise ship, Aurora, sank on the coral reef, divers found that coral had _____ over almost the whole surface of the ship.

10. There are several things that you can do with your house which will _____ its value, for example converting the loft into living space.

11. dare

Put the most suitable word in each space. Think about the part of speech required in each space. Make sure you use the correct form.

additive, condone, data, date, donate, dowry, edit, endowment, extradite, mandate, render, tradition

1. In some countries, when a woman gets married, her parents must give a large _____ of money or goods to the groom's parents.
2. We've received an invoice from a catering company for services _____ on Friday 25th January. Do you know anything about it?
3. The government has applied to the high court in Russia to _____ the three men suspected of last month's £50 million bank robbery in London.
4. I understand why you hit the other player after he kicked you, but as the manager, I can't _____ violent behaviour. You're out of the team.
5. If I win the competition I'm going to _____ half the money to the local children's hospital to help them buy new medical equipment.
6. We're receiving some really fascinating _____ about the surface of Mars from the Mars Explorer vehicle, which successfully landed there yesterday.
7. The problem with packaged food these days is that it's full of _____ and preservatives, which have been found to affect children's behaviour.
8. The Prime Minister is expected today to set the _____ for the general election, with May 5th the most likely one, according to political analysts.
9. After you've written the wedding speech, let me see it in case there is anything in it that I need to _____ out. We don't want to offend anyone.
10. It's been a family _____ for over two hundred years that the eldest daughter gets married with her mother's wedding ring.
11. As the Minister for Overseas Development, I am _____ with the task of organising the new African development fund.
12. We've decided to put £100 a month into a special fund to give each of our children an _____ when they reach the age of eighteen.

12. dicere 1

Put the most suitable word in each space. Think about the part of speech required in each space. Make sure you use the correct form.

abdicate, condition, contradict, dedicate, dictate, dictation, diction, dictum, ditto, ditty, edict, verdict

1. OK, everyone. Can you all put your textbooks away and open your exercise books on a blank page? I'm going to give you a _____. Ready?

2. The atmosphere in the courtroom was tense as the jury came in and sat down. Then the judge asked them for their _____: guilty!

3. The bank has decided to lend you the money, but because the risk is higher than usual, there are some special _____ that you have to meet.

4. If I tell the children they can't have any sweets, and then you tell them that they can, it confuses them. We must stop _____ each other all the time.

5. Did you hear the speech that Emily gave at the school open day? She didn't use to be a good speaker, but now she's really improved her _____.

6. I would like to _____ the next song to the late, great John Lennon, whose wonderful work inspired me to start writing songs.

7. You shouldn't allow your husband to _____ to you how your marriage should work. You're both equal partners. Try to stand up for yourself.

8. The President today issued an emergency _____ that all towns and cities in the path of the hurricane should be evacuated immediately.

9. I've just remembered this little _____ that my mum used to sing to me as a boy when she was happy. I still remember the words. It goes like this.

10. I know you didn't plan for this baby, but the fact is your girlfriend's pregnant and you can't _____ your responsibility to her. Just face up to it.

11. The new manager wants to change the work system, but it works fine. I always go by the old _____: if it isn't broken, don't fix it.

12. I'm sorry, but I won't be around to help you do the shopping this weekend because I'm busy at work, _____ next weekend and the weekend after.

13. dicere 2

Put the most suitable word in each space. Think about the part of speech required in each space. Make sure you use the correct form.

addiction, dictionary, index, indicate, indication, indicative, indict, interdict, predicament, predicate, predict, vindicate

1. This medicine is _____ for general domestic use and can only be used in a hospital environment. You'll need a doctor's prescription to get it.

2. If you need to find a particular word, look it up in the _____ at the back of the book and it will tell you the page that it appears on.

3. The government's whole argument is _____ on the false idea that people react to a threat in the same way, but everyone reacts differently.

4. After twenty years of trying to give up drugs, the singer, Harry Ball, finally beat his _____, and wrote about it in his new book, Up and Down.

5. It's very difficult to _____ the future direction of the world economy at the best of times, so don't believe anyone who claims to be sure about it.

6. Remember during your driving test to check on your mirror and _____ clearly the direction that you want to take before you turn.

7. We thought we were in a really bad _____, in the middle of the desert with the car broken down and little food and water, but luckily we were soon rescued.

8. The children's aggressive behaviour in the playground is _____ of their lack of respect for each other and for society in general.

9. Professor Jenkins has always claimed that his theory is right, and these new discoveries have confirmed it and absolutely _____ him.

10. Colin White, the merchant banker, was today _____ on charges of embezzling $5 million from his bank. He will appear in court tomorrow.

11. I always carry around a pocket _____ when I'm travelling in another country in case I come across any words that I don't understand.

12. The latest results from our opinion poll give no _____ of any loss of support for the government, despite the worsening economic situation.

14. duo

Put the most suitable word in each space. Think about the part of speech required in each space. Make sure you use the correct form.

double, doublet, dozen, dual, duel, duet, duo, duplicate, duplicitous, redouble

1. Cynthia and Dave sang a beautiful _____ at the school concert last night. They've got fantastic voices.

2. If you lose your identity card, it will cost you £10 to get a _____, so keep it in a safe place.

3. As soon as the paparazzi found out who the prince's new girlfriend was, _____ of them rushed to her house to try to photograph her.

4. "Fashion" is actually a _____ of the word "faction", although they have very different meanings in modern English.

5. Stan Laurel and Oliver Hardy, who made numerous films together, are probably the best known and loved comedy _____ in the history of entertainment.

6. In this game, if you throw a _____ six on the dice, you can take another throw after your move.

7. In the old days, if one man insulted another, it was common for them to fight a _____ with pistols or swords to defend their honour.

8. After a day searching for the lost children in the local woods, the police said they would _____ their efforts to find them before dark.

9. Ron was born in Canada, but came to Britain when he was five, so he has _____ nationality and he can work in Europe or America.

10. You can't trust what Sheila says. She's so _____ that she'll even tell her husband one thing and then tell her mother the exact opposite.

15. facere 1

Put the most suitable word in each space. Think about the part of speech required in each space. Make sure you use the correct form.

affect, affectation, affection, affectionate, defect, defection, defective, deficiency, deficit, disaffected, effective, efficient

1. The workers went on strike because they felt extremely _____ after the management promised them a 5% pay rise, but gave them only 2%.

2. After losing five games in a row, the manager introduced a new system for the team, which proved so _____ that they won their next five games.

3. Colin proposed to Helen, but she refused him. She said she had a lot of _____ for him, but didn't love him enough to marry him.

4. At the moment the trade figures show a _____ of about $5 billion. The country needs to export far more to balance it up and get into a surplus.

5. The government's slim majority of seven in Parliament was reduced even further after the _____ of two of its MPs to the opposition.

6. I've been very tired and listless recently, so I went to the doctor. He said I have a vitamin _____ and gave me a prescription to get some vitamins.

7. Since Tom's wife left him, it has _____ him a great deal. He stays at home all the time and rarely sees his friends. He really needs to get over it.

8. We are looking for a keen, skilled, experienced and _____ manager who can run a whole department and organise a large team of workers.

9. Noel really annoys me when he speaks with those French _____ in his accent, as if he grew up in Paris and not in London.

10. The Humbrow toy Company has recalled over ten thousand of its Cuddly Carrie dolls after a serious design _____ was discovered.

11. Well, that's a surprise. Tibby's usually a very timid cat with strangers, but she's being very _____ to you. She really seems to like you.

12. After May was born, doctors discovered she had a _____ heart valve, so they had to operate immediately. As you see, she's recovered well.

16. facere 2

Put the most suitable word in each space. Think about the part of speech required in each space. Make sure you use the correct form.

facile, facsimile, fact, faction, factor, factory, factual, faculty, fashion, feasible, feat, feature

1. There were various _____ which contributed to the plane crash, but the crucial one was the bad weather when the plane was coming in to land.

2. This political party has split into two main _____; one wants to stay in the European Union, and the other wants to leave.

3. The way Jamie plays tennis is so _____. It seems like he's not using any effort or energy, but he gets such powerful and accurate shots.

4. I think he's guilty. The _____ speak for themselves; the victim's blood was on his shirt and he was seen leaving the house right after the murder.

5. Have you met Prof Roberts? He's just joined the Physics _____ at the university to teach Particle Physics on the postgraduate course.

6. One of the strangest _____ of a hurricane is the eye of the storm, right at the centre, where the winds are very light and the air is clear.

7. The Kawahama Car Company is going to open a new _____ in Compton, creating around 500 new jobs for the local community.

8. I saw Alien Invasion last night. It's a really good film. This astronaut comes home to his wife, acting in a strange _____, sort of in a trance.

9. I read this book called The Uttermost Part of the World, a _____ account of the first Europeans in Tierra del Fuego and the indigenous tribes.

10. Your business plan looks good, but in reality it's just not _____. We would need to spend double the amount money that we have for it to work.

11. This picture that Morris painted is an exact _____ of the one in the art gallery. How did he manage to produce such a faithful, accurate copy?

12. Captain James received a medal for bravery after he rescued a wounded comrade under fire. It was a truly heroic _____ of courage in battle.

17. facere 3

Put the most suitable word in each space. Think about the part of speech required in each space. Make sure you use the correct form.

affair, benefit, confectionery, confetti, effect, efficacious, office, official, officious, profit, profiteering, refectory

1. I'm doing all this work for your _____, not mine, so the least you could do is to thank me for it. After all, you're going to be a lot better off.

2. After the wedding party left the church, the ground was left absolutely covered in the _____ that the guests had thrown over the happy couple.

3. There have been a lot of rumours about the princess being pregnant, but now it's _____, after an announcement by the prince's private secretary.

4. The value of the housing market has grown so much that people who bought a house ten years ago can sell at a huge _____.

5. An analysis of kitchen cleaning products shows that new, improved Sparkle is the most _____, with the best results of the ten products tested.

6. I have to go and see the principal, so you if go to the college _____ and get lunch for us, I'll meet there you in ten minutes.

7. The shop sells all kinds of _____, including chocolate, mints, sweets and crisps.

8. Here is the news. The former Prime Minister, Hugh Daley, has died. He was 88. He held _____ as Prime Minister for six years, from 1965 to 1971.

9. The three climbers who had been lost in bad weather on Mount Misty yesterday were found alive today. They showed no serious physical _____.

10. You have no right to talk to people about me behind my back. Just keep out of my personal _____. They're none of your business.

11. During the last war there was a big shortage of everyday goods, like cigarettes and alcohol. Tom's father made a lot of money through _____.

12. The guy on the nightclub door is so _____. Just because he's wearing a uniform, he thinks he can boss everyone about and tell them what to do.

18. facere 4

Put the most suitable word in each space. Think about the part of speech required in each space. Make sure you use the correct form.

counterfeit, defeat, difficult, disinfectant, forfeit, infect, manufacture, perfect, prefect, proficient, suffice, surfeit

1. Hang on! This twenty pound note isn't real. Are you trying to pass me _____ money? I'm going to call the police.

2. Scientists investigating cases of foot and mouth disease in Hampshire have found ten cows which have been _____ with the disease.

3. You have to use up the rest of your vacation time before August 31st or you'll _____ it. You can't carry it over to next year.

4. Great news! Our company has won an order to _____ a new type of computer chip. This is our chance to really expand and open new markets.

5. Although Jim Robinson suffered the first _____ in his boxing career against Austin Leonard, he's going to get the chance to win back his title.

6. This job's far too _____ for one person to do alone. I really need some help, or I won't be able to do it.

7. If I were you, I'd take the new job in the Paris office. It's the _____ opportunity for you to learn French and get to know France.

8. Because of the exceptionally good weather, there's a _____ of strawberries in the shops going really cheap. They just can't sell them all.

9. The whole house is really filthy. Nobody's cleaned it for ages. We'll need to use _____ to make sure everything is really clean and germfree.

10. We've invited around a hundred people to the wedding, so I think around thirty bottles of champagne should _____ for the wedding toast.

11. This is going to be a difficult case to win, but with James Hanley, you'll have a good chance. He's the most _____ lawyer in the country and rarely loses.

12. I was made a _____ at school because I was such a good student. I had to take charge of the class when the teacher went out.

19. finis

Put the most suitable word in each space. Think about the part of speech required in each space. Make sure you use the correct form.

affinity, confine, definition, final, finance, finery, finesse, finish, finite, infinitesimal, infinity, refine

1. Jenny wasn't hurt in the car crash, but she's badly shaken up. The doctors have _____ her to bed for a few days to give her time to recover.

2. We need to be far more careful with our _____. If we don't cut down on our spending we're going to run out of money very soon.

3. I went to pick Ann up to take her to the dance. The door opened and there she stood, dressed in all her _____. She looked absolutely amazing.

4. This paint is quite expensive, but it will give your wood a really beautiful, shiny, gloss _____ after it dries.

5. Plutonium is such a toxic material that it takes only a few milligrams of it, an absolutely _____ amount, to kill a person.

6. After the sugar is extracted from the cane, it is _____ in the factory and packed, ready to be sent to the shops.

7. A good dictionary will not just give you the _____ of a word, but also its pronunciation and examples of its use.

8. This is Henderson's _____ attempt at 2 metres in the high jump competition. He failed on his other jumps, so he has to get this one, or he's out.

9. The universe is so big that many people believe that it has no end and stretches away into _____.

10. Although there is a _____ number of words in a language, there is no limit to amount of sentences that those words can create.

11. During the card game, Joel Foster managed to _____ all of the other players' moves with such skill that he won all their money.

12. I met Joan at a friend's party. We realised we had a great _____ for each other and shared a lot of interests. The relationship just took off from there.

20. frangere

Put the most suitable word in each space. Think about the part of speech required in each space. Make sure you use the correct form.

defragment, diffract, fraction, fractious, fracture, fragile, fragment, fragmentary, frail, infraction, infringe, refract

1. Tony was arrested for being drunk, but the police decided that it was a minor
    _____, so they let him go without charging him with anything.

2. Don't let the children come in here. A vase fell on the floor and broke, and there
    are lots of _____ everywhere. I'm trying to clean them all up.

3. When light shines through a prism, it gets _____ into all the
    colours of the rainbow. It's really beautiful.

4. It's time for Jimmy to go to bed. He's been up for far too long. When he gets tired
    he gets very _____ and kicks and screams all the way to bed.

5. I'm really angry. I did a lot of work for this agency, but they paid me only a
    _____ of the money that they promised. I want the rest.

6. If the hard disk on your computer is running really slowly, you should
    _____ it because your data is not stored in an organised way.

7. I don't think you should send these wine glasses in the post. They're far too
    _____ and you can't trust the postal workers to handle them
    carefully.

8. My grandmother turned 90 last week. We had a big party for her. Although she's
    very _____ now, she still got up and danced.

9. You have to be very careful when driving these days. If you _____
    the speed limit and get caught on camera, you could end up paying a big fine.

10. At the moment we have a very _____ knowledge of this ancient
    civilisation. These new archaeological finds will give us a much clearer picture.

11. The car accident looked absolutely awful, but I only suffered a double
    _____ of my left leg. I was really lucky to escape further injury.

12. If you put a stick in water, it looks bent because the water _____
    the light as it travels through the surface.

21. genus, gignere 1

All these words are adjectives. Put the most suitable adjective in each space.

benign, congenial, congenital, general, generic, generous, genial, genital, genteel, gentle, genuine, malignant

1. My mother's gone into hospital for tests on a tumour in her stomach. If it's
    _____, it may be cancer and she'll need an operation.
2. You can use a _____ password to access the computer system
    until you get registered on the system tomorrow. Then you'll get your own one.
3. All the classes in our language school are taught in a relaxed, friendly and
    _____ atmosphere, which helps the students learn better.
4. Experts examined the painting in detail and found it was a _____
    Picasso and not a fake or a copy. It could be worth millions of dollars.
5. Health officials are worried about the spread of _____ diseases,
    owing to the increase in unprotected sex among young people.
6. This club has existed for over 200 years, so all applicants must demonstrate
    their good character to ensure its distinguished and _____
    atmosphere.
7. I would like to thank Mr Clark of Clark Enterprises for his _____
    donation of £1000 to our youth club. It is very much appreciated.
8. Because our son was born with _____ heart disease, he'll need an
    operation to repair it, or maybe even a heart transplant.
9. After a lively discussion about expanding our membership, the
    _____ feeling among the delegates was that we should invite new
    members to join.
10. Despite the basic conditions and very few luxuries at the children's home, the
    children were healthy and their treatment was relatively _____.
11. What a beautiful day! Sun, sea and sand, with a _____ breeze
    off the sea to keep the heat off. What more could you ask for on a holiday?
12. When I first met Tony, I immediately noticed he how _____ he is.
    He's got such a friendly and easy manner that he gets on well with everyone.

22. genus, gignere 2

All these words are nouns. Put the most suitable noun in each space. Make sure you use the plural where necessary.

engine, gender, genitive, genius, genre, gentleman, gentry, genus, miscegenation, primogeniture, progenitor, progeny

1. Scientists have discovered a new type of cat in the mountains of South America. It may even be an entirely new _____.

2. Every May in this small country, an important and popular festival is held in which people celebrate the lives of their _____ from long ago.

3. You really should read this book. I've never read anything like it. It's a work of pure _____, the best of its kind. You won't find a better writer.

4. It's important to remember when writing for a living that there are many different _____ of writing and you need to operate in the correct one.

5. In the past, steel production was the main _____ of the economy, but now most plants have closed and the industry has virtually ceased to exist.

6. When the Europeans first arrived in South America, _____ between Europeans and locals was very common and produced a new mixed race.

7. My new boyfriend's family is part of the _____. They have a house in the centre of London and huge country house in Devon. They're really rich.

8. The only grammatical case to survive from Old English into Modern English is the _____, which is indicated by an apostrophe and "s".

9. When my grandfather died aged 98, his _____ included twenty grandchildren, and seven great grandchildren.

10. The question of _____ equality in this country is still important, as many working women don't get the same pay and conditions as men.

11. Mr Simpkins next door is a real _____. He's never rude and always treats everyone with kindness and respect.

12. Because of the law of _____, the king's eldest son always becomes the next king.

23. genus, gignere 3

Put the most suitable word in each space. Think about the part of speech required in each space. Make sure you use the correct form.

degenerate, disingenuous, engender, generalise, generate, gentrify, impregnate, indigenous, ingenious, ingenuous, pregnant, regenerate

1. I thought I could trust Colin. He seemed to be very honest and sincere, but he was actually really _____. It was all an act, a big pretence.

2. You can buy this new type of plaster which is already _____ with antiseptic, so that you can put it directly on a wound without having to clean it.

3. Before Europeans arrived on this island the _____ population was over five thousand, but in fifty years it fell to a few hundred through disease.

4. The market for our company's current products is not growing much, so we need to find new ways to _____ income and grow as a company.

5. The problem with politicians today is that people don't think that they tell the truth. It's very difficult for politicians to _____ trust in themselves.

6. We were thinking of ways for our new band to get publicity and Jim came up with a really _____ plan to give away our first CD free for one weekend.

7. Relations between these two countries have _____ so much that there is a real danger of war breaking out between them.

8. Just because you had a bad experience with one particular teacher, you can't _____ and say they're all bad. Most of them are decent.

9. This area used to be untidy and run down with old houses, but now it's being _____ and a lot of middle class and affluent people are moving in.

10. As the President stepped in front of the microphone, the atmosphere among the audience was _____ with expectation about what he would say.

11. Young children are so _____ that they often believe anything that older people tell them, even if it there's no truth in it at all.

12. Since the last coal mine closed, the government has spent a lot of money to _____ this area with new housing, jobs, schools and businesses.

24. nasci

Put the most suitable word in each space. Think about the part of speech required in each space. Make sure you use the correct form.

international, naïve, natal, nation, national, nationalise, native, natural, naturalise, nature, renaissance, supernatural

1. The government has announced that it intends to _____ the railway company to save it from bankruptcy because it is losing so much money.
2. Although Jonah's a really big dog, he's actually got a very sweet, docile _____. The kids play with him all the time and he doesn't mind.
3. I really don't believe it when food companies claim their products are completely _____. After all, they're all made in factories and put in packets.
4. Often when something strange happens which can't be easily explained, people think that it's a _____ phenomenon, like a ghost or spirit.
5. As a boy I was very _____ with people and thought they were all fair and honest, but now I know it's better not to trust people you don't know.
6. The _____ language in this country is Creole, but most people also speak English well, as it is taught in schools from an early age.
7. Here is the news. The President is getting ready to make his annual address to the _____, so we'll go live to the Presidential Palace in a minute.
8. If you live in this country continuously for more than five years, you can become _____ and apply for citizenship.
9. Jimmy Spooner has been playing so well for his club that the England coach has included him in the team for the next _____ game with Germany.
10. The _____ government has promised to make a new law to give the regional governments more power to run their own affairs.
11. After many years of poor conditions and falling crowds, football has experienced a _____ as money has come into the game and crowds have grown.
12. Nowadays, fewer babies and mothers are dying during childbirth, owing to the huge improvements in _____ care.

25. gradi, gradus 1

Put the most suitable word in each space. Think about the part of speech required in each space. Make sure you use the correct form.

aggressive, congress, degrade, degree, digress, downgrade, gradation, regression, transgress, upgrade

1. When you are giving a talk, you should stick to your subject and try not to _____. You might lose your audience's interest.

2. If you look at the painting carefully you can see the _____ in colour from light to shade, from one side of the picture to the other.

3. The system of government is made up of a president and a _____, which is itself made up of representatives elected by each state.

4. Timmy's behaviour has been very good lately, but I'm concerned that he's showing signs of _____ to his previous bad behaviour.

5. If you buy this new computer programme now, you will be able to get a free _____ to the next version after a year.

6. The police managed to collect evidence from crime scene, but much of it had _____ too much over time to be of any use.

7. If you _____ any of the rules of the organisation, you are liable to lose your membership.

8. Alf's a really nice guy to know as a person, but when he gets on the football field he becomes far too _____. He needs to control himself more.

9. At the moment the new Prime Minister is enjoying a very high _____ of popularity, but it might not last if he doesn't cut taxes soon.

10. Hurricane Gladys, which had threatened the islands of the Caribbean, has weakened and has been _____ from category four to category three.

26. gradi, gradus 2

Put the most suitable word in each space. Think about the part of speech required in each space. Make sure you use the correct form.

grade, gradient, gradual, graduate, ingredient, postgraduate, progress, progression, progressive, retrograde

1. When this government was first elected, they had many _____ ideas, like free health care, better public transport and new public housing programmes.

2. I really don't know how Terry managed to _____ from university. He did hardly any work in his final year, but he still passed all his final exams.

3. Scientists predict that over the next fifty years there will be a _____ increase in global temperatures of up to 2 degrees.

4. When I go shopping, I always have to check the _____ listed on the packet to see what's in the food, because my son is allergic to nuts.

5. You've made a lot of _____ in your work and I'm very pleased. If you continue in this way, I'm confident you'll pass all your exams.

6. If you leave your course, it will be a _____ step in your career. You should complete it first and then decide what to do.

7. I want to talk to you about your career _____ after you finish this course. You can do another course, or there are various jobs you can apply for.

8. When I finish my first degree at university this year, I haven't decided whether to find a job or take a _____ course and get a higher degree.

9. This hill has such a steep _____ that you have to stay in first gear to drive all the way to the top.

10. If you really want to go to university you'll need to work much harder to get the required _____ in your exams.

27. gravis

Put the most suitable word in each space. Think about the part of speech required in each space. Make sure you use the correct form.

aggravate, aggrieve, grave, gravitas, gravitate, gravity, grief, grievance, grieve, grievous

1. The robber hit the shopkeeper on the head with a metal bar and seriously injured him. When he was arrested, he was charged with _____ bodily harm.

2. After the divorce Tom felt very _____, since his ex-wife managed to keep the house and most of the money, and he was left with very little.

3. The laws of _____ mean that if you throw something up in the air it will always come down to earth again.

4. The doctor walked slowly into the living room with a very _____ look on his face, and everyone knew immediately that our father had died.

5. A lot of people at the party _____ to the kitchen to eat and chat because the music in the living room was so loud.

6. After Billy's dog died, he was full of sadness and _____ for weeks, and only came out of it when we bought him another dog.

7. If you have a complaint or a _____ of any sort against the college, you have to fill in a form and it will be sent to the management for consideration.

8. The ex-president was an immensely important figure in world politics and maintained an air of _____ and respect everywhere he went.

9. In many countries, people wear black clothes for months to show that they are _____ after the death of a member of the family.

10. You need to rest your leg and not play for a couple of weeks, or you might _____ the injury and it will take longer for you to recover.

28. jungere

Put the most suitable word in each space. Think about the part of speech required in each space. Make sure you use the correct form.

adjoining, conjoined, conjugal, conjunction, disjointed, enjoin, injunction, join, joint, junction, juncture, rejoinder

1. I broke Mum's new plate, but I managed to repair it with some superglue. Look! You can't even see the _____.

2. Doctors are now performing an operation to separate the twins who were born _____ at the head last week.

3. After the widespread destruction from the storm, the army worked hard in _____ with the police and fire services to clear up the wreckage.

4. The High Court has issued an immediate _____ to prevent newspapers from publishing extracts from the prince's private diaries.

5. The team just didn't play well. Their organisation was _____ and the players found it difficult to get a good rhythm. That's why they lost.

6. The leader _____ upon his followers to stay true to their beliefs and not to lose faith in the cause, no matter what difficulties they would face.

7. Francis asked his wife for a divorce because he claimed she had refused him his _____ rights as a husband.

8. It doesn't matter what you say to Ted. He always comes back with a witty _____, which makes everyone laugh.

9. Usually when people get married, they open a _____ bank account so that they can take care of their finances together.

10. At this _____, although the talks are continuing, it's difficult to say whether they could break down or continue until both sides reach an agreement.

11. After the gas explosion destroyed our house, the police decided to evacuate the _____ houses for safety reasons.

12. Continue along this road for the next five kilometres until you come to a _____. Take the right turn and go another five kilometres.

29. lavare, luere

Put the most suitable word in each space. Think about the part of speech required in each space. Make sure you use the correct form.

ablution, alluvial, deluge, dilute, launder, laundry, lavatory, lavish (2), lotion

1. This is the last clean shirt that I've got. Can you take all the clothes to the _____ today and get them washed?

2. In one day, the storm _____ the town with more rain than it usually got in a month, leading to severe flooding.

3. That's a horrible rash you've got on your arm. Rub this _____ into it every day and it should be gone in a week.

4. I'm afraid you'll have to stop all your _____ spending on clothes and holidays and start taking care of your money. You've almost used it all up.

5. You can't just drink the juice straight from the bottle like that because it's concentrated. You have to _____ it with water first.

6. The police are investigating the company's activities after accusations of money _____ from illegal gambling and drug dealing.

7. The _____ soils in this river estuary are particularly rich and ideal for farming.

8. Can you wait for a few minutes? I just need to go to the _____ and freshen up before we eat.

9. After the monks get up in the morning they perform their _____, say their prayers and eat their breakfast in silence.

10. All the cinema critics _____ huge praise on Vanessa Healey for her wonderful performance in her latest film, Highway to Hell.

30. levis

Put the most suitable word in each space. Think about the part of speech required in each space. Make sure you use the correct form.

alleviate, elevate, elevator, leaven, lever, leverage, levitate, levity, levy, relevant, relief, relieve

1. At the end of the show the magician _____ himself off the ground. I couldn't see any ropes or wires, so I don't know how he did it.
2. How can you laugh in a situation like this? I don't think you realise how serious things are. This is no time for _____.
3. When you've mixed the flour and water to make dough, you have to add yeast to _____ the bread mix before you put it in the oven to bake.
4. Oh! Thank goodness! Here's my wallet on the table with all my credit cards and money. What a _____! I thought I had dropped it in the street.
5. Jenny's got a broken leg and two broken ribs. I've given her an injection to _____ the pain, but we need to get her to hospital soon.
6. The problem with football today is that the richer clubs have so much more _____ than the smaller ones when important decisions are made.
7. Can you read this form carefully and fill in the _____ information, such as your name, address, age and experience?
8. Take the _____ to the fourth floor. Mr Clark's office is the third room on the left.
9. The government has decided to increase the _____ on tobacco by another 5%. That means 70% of the price of a packet of cigarettes is tax.
10. To open the door in an emergency, lift the _____ and push hard on the door.
11. When you've finished your lunch break, can you go and _____ Steve on the main door? He's been on duty since 8.00 this morning and needs a break.
12. As a result of the continuing flu epidemic, the issue of public health has been _____ to the top of the government's agenda.

31. locus

Put the most suitable word in each space. Think about the part of speech required in each space. Make sure you use the correct form.

allocate, collocate, dislocate, lieu, lieutenant, local, locale, localised, locality, locate, location, relocate

1. We've got a serious problem with staff shortages, with so many people off sick. If you work on Saturday, you can have a day off in _____.
2. I _____ my shoulder playing rugby last week. It was really painful, but the hospital doctor put it back in and it's getting better.
3. Although there has been a lot of rain recently and many rivers have risen, the flooding seems to be _____ in a few places and not widespread.
4. We left our bags in our hotel room and went to the _____ pub for a drink. The atmosphere was really nice and the people were really friendly.
5. The most important thing to think about when you buy a new house is the _____. You don't want to buy in a bad area.
6. Following the disappearance of the lone round-the-world sailor, Peter Cargill, searchers have _____ his boat in the South Atlantic near St Helena.
7. Police have _____ all the sightings of the missing schoolgirl Emma Francis and it seems that she has been taken from London to Glasgow.
8. On the staff development day, each of us was _____ to a team, which had to work together to be the first to solve a problem and win a prize.
9. It's nice living here in the country, but the only problem is that there are no shops in the _____, so I have to drive two miles to the supermarket.
10. The manager said that our company is closing the Bristol office and we're all to be _____ to Edinburgh in Scotland, but I don't want to move.
11. My son's just been promoted to the rank of _____ in his army regiment. We're going to the ceremony tomorrow.
12. Police searched the immediate _____ where the body was found and took away some items of evidence which they found.

32. ludere

Put the most suitable word in each space. Think about the part of speech required in each space. Make sure you use the correct form.

allude, collude, delude, delusional, disillusion, elude, elusive, illusion, illusory, interlude, ludicrous, prelude

1. If you keep your eyes open as we walk through the jungle, you may just see a cocrico if you're lucky, but they're very shy and _____ birds.

2. You're a good footballer, but don't _____ yourself into thinking that you can play professionally. You need to reach a far better standard to do that.

3. There's going to be a short _____ before the next group goes on stage to play, so we can go to the bar for a quick drink.

4. These talks between the two companies are just a _____ to a major merger between them, which is planned for next month.

5. Robertson was regarded as a hero after the war, until evidence emerged that he had _____ with the enemy to protect his business interests.

6. I've applied for promotion four times in this job and been refused each time, so I'm completely _____ with this company and I want to leave.

7. In his speech the Prime Minister _____ to a possible rise in interest rates, while not actually stating categorically that they would go up.

8. In the film The Producers, an accountant and a theatre producer come up with up a _____ plan to deliberately put on a play they know will fail.

9. I think your grandmother is _____. She thinks that I'm your father and not your husband. I mean, I don't even look like your father.

10. If you look at both these straight lines, one of them looks longer than the other, but actually it's an optical _____. They're exactly the same.

11. Do you remember the guy who stayed in the room opposite us at university? His name _____ me, but I saw him yesterday in the library.

12. Some religions claim that everything that we see, hear and experience is actually _____, and that reality lies elsewhere waiting to be discovered.

33. medius

Put the most suitable word in each space. Think about the part of speech required in each space. Make sure you use the correct form.

immediate, intermediary, intermediate, mean, media, mediate, medieval, mediocre, Mediterranean, medium, meridian, mezzanine

1. This cathedral was first built 800 years ago in _____ times and has stood here ever since, though it has undergone occasional repairs.
2. I've looked at your reading and writing test and I think it would be best to put you in the _____ English class for now. If you improve you can go up.
3. It's obvious that you two aren't going to settle this disagreement easily or quickly, so I think it's best if I _____ between you and help you settle it.
4. Mary Jackson has been called the best singer of the past few years, but her voice is rather _____ and lacks the range and power of a truly great singer.
5. The latest government figures show that the _____ annual salary in this country has risen by 5% over the last two years to £25,000.
6. The problem with the _____ these days, especially the tabloid press, is that they're not interested in real stories, only scandals and celebrities.
7. We've decided to take a holiday somewhere hot this year, probably on the _____ coast of France or Spain.
8. That woman claims she's a spiritual _____ and has made contact with the spirit of my dead mother, but I don't believe in any of that stuff at all.
9. The great thing about doing business on the Internet is that you can sell your products directly to your customers and not through an _____.
10. Men's clothes are up on the _____ floor of the store, along with children's clothes and shoes, and women's clothes are on the first floor.
11. Any further misuse of the company's electronic communications system will result in _____ dismissal. You have been warned.
12. The _____ passes right through this spot. You can stand over it with one leg in the west and one in the east.

34. memor

Put the most suitable word in each space. Think about the part of speech required in each space. Make sure you use the correct form.

commemorate, memorabilia, memoirs, memorable, memorandum, memorial, memorise, memory, remember, remembrance

1. When politicians leave office they can usually make a lot of money by writing and publishing their _____ of their years in government.

2. The second Sunday in November is known as _____ Sunday, which is held to honour the people who died in the world wars.

3. Internal messages in an organisation used to be sent in the form of a paper _____, but now virtually all companies use email.

4. My parents had their diamond wedding anniversary yesterday. The whole family came. It was such a _____ occasion for all of us.

5. I've managed to _____ a few quotes from the play we studied in class, so that I can write them in the English Literature exam.

6. Next week is the thousandth anniversary of the founding of our city, so we're going to have a big street festival to _____ it.

7. Jim is a real football fanatic. He's filled his house with posters, shirts and all kinds of other _____ from his favourite team.

8. Can you _____ what to buy at the supermarket, or do you need to write it down? I don't want you to forget anything.

9. Have you seen my keys anywhere? I'm sure I left them here on the table when I came in. Maybe I'm losing my _____.

10. The statue in front of our office building is a _____ to Sir James Morrison, who founded our company two hundred years ago.

35. minus

Put the most suitable word in each space. Think about the part of speech required in each space. Make sure you use the correct form.

administer, diminish, minimal, minimise, minimum, minister, ministry, minor, minority, minus, minuscule, minute

1. The total sum we'll get from the house sale is £250,000, _____ the fees for the solicitor and estate agent, which leaves us with about £246,000.

2. If the glacier on this mountain continues to _____ as a result of global warming, in twenty years there'll be nothing left of it at all.

3. The fact is that these days most football fans in this country are generally well-behaved and it's only a small _____ that causes all the trouble.

4. At the end of each month you can either pay off the full balance on your credit card, or just pay the _____ amount, which is 2% of the balance.

5. The Foreign Secretary, Geoffrey Major, has announced that he is to give up his job as a government _____ to spend more time with his family.

6. A coach has crashed on the high street today. Fifteen people were treated for shock and _____ injuries, but no one was seriously hurt.

7. An important part of a hospital nurse's job is to check the patients' condition on a regular basis and _____ medicine when required.

8. After searching the murder suspect's flat, police found _____ quantities of the victim's blood on the carpet, and they are now analysing it.

9. The government has decided to create a new _____ combining education and family affairs, which should run much more smoothly than now.

10. When I started university my finances were _____, barely enough to live on, so I had to get a part-time job to provide me with extra money to spend.

11. The new double-glazed windows should _____ the noise from the busy road outside so that you can have some peace and quiet.

12. When you stand at the top of a tall building, the people down below look so _____, they're almost like ants.

36. modus

Put the most suitable word in each space. Think about the part of speech required in each space. Make sure you use the correct form.

accommodate, commodity, mode, model, modem, moderate, modern, modest, modicum, modify, modulate, module

1. World prices of _____ like coffee, sugar and orange juice, are continuing to rise following poor harvests, so expect to pay more in the shops.
2. The latest broadband internet _____ that we can supply now has download speeds of up to 20mbs.
3. Before we start, please make sure you either switch off your mobile phone or put it into silent _____. I don't want anything disturbing our meeting.
4. It's difficult to make a lot of money from running a shop these days. I make a _____ profit, enough to keep going, but I'd love to make more.
5. I'm terribly sorry, but we'll have to _____ your travel arrangements because the flight you wanted to take is fully booked. The earliest one is tomorrow.
6. We're looking for a hotel which can _____ a party of 50 people. Can you take that many in your hotel?
7. James is a _____ student. He always does his work on time, takes an active part in class and helps less able students. I'm very pleased with him.
8. Tanya has such a fantastic voice that she can _____ it with ease, regardless of how difficult the song is that she's singing.
9. This computer course consists of six _____. You study three in the first semester and the other three in the second semester.
10. I don't really like _____ furniture. It's so plain. I much prefer to look around antique shops and buy something older, with character and style.
11. Although Norman seemed to be calm and composed on the surface, I detected a _____ of fear in his voice as he spoke; not much, but it's there.
12. The government today published the latest inflation figures. There has been a _____ increase, but not enough to cause alarm.

37. munus

Put the most suitable word in each space. Think about the part of speech required in each space. Make sure you use the correct form.

common, commons, communal, commune, communicate, communion, community, excommunicate, immunity, incommunicado, municipal, remuneration

1. I'm really worried about my son. He's stopped studying and left college to join a new-age _____ in the country and doesn't want to see us again.

2. The local priest refused to perform church services according to the designated format, so the church authorities _____ him.

3. The police promised Simpson _____ from prosecution if he told them the names of the other bank robbers and testified against them.

4. The British parliament consists of two houses, the House of Lords and the House of _____, which has 646 Members of Parliament.

5. The employment law clearly states that if a man and a woman do the same type of job, then they should receive the same _____.

6. When Rick met Louis a year ago at a friend's party, they soon realised they had a lot in _____ and it was the beginning of a beautiful friendship.

7. The students each have a room with a bed, a study table and a wash basin. There's also a kitchen and a _____ area to meet in.

8. The best way to educate young people and keep them out of trouble is for the government to work in _____ with local authorities and youth groups.

9. Hans can speak enough English to _____ on an everyday level, but he needs to learn a lot more before he can study at university here.

10. I'm taking the phone off the hook so no one can call me. I've got so much work to do, I need to be _____ for a few hours.

11. The local government has had to cut back on its _____ and building works because it has run out of money.

12. The local _____ is made up of people and families from many different countries, but relations between them are generally very good.

38. parare

Put the most suitable word in each space. Think about the part of speech required in each space. Make sure you use the correct form.

apparatus, disparate, disrepair, irreparable, pare, prepare, repair, reparation, separate, sever, several, severance

1. With the growing crisis between the two countries, the governments decided to _____ all diplomatic relations between them immediately.

2. The problem is, since my husband lost his job, we've had to _____ our expenses right down to the minimum, so no holidays or nights out for now.

3. At the end of the First World War, Germany was forced to pay huge _____ to other countries to cover their losses during the war.

4. Sorry, but we can do nothing with your car. The damage is _____. If I were you, I'd sell it for scrap and get a new one with the insurance payout.

5. The extra money that the school has received has enabled us to buy new science equipment, including the new _____ in the physics laboratory.

6. A great manager in any sport is someone who can make a strong team out of the _____ skills and abilities of all the players.

7. When we first saw the house, it was in a state of total _____, but we loved the location so much we decided to buy it and renovate it.

8. When the new management took over the company, a lot of people lost their jobs, but each got a very good _____ payment of over £20,000.

9. At first their marriage was good, but it started to go wrong after only two years, and finally they decided to _____ for a while.

10. Come on! We have to get down to work quickly. We've only got three hours to _____ for the party tonight. I'll clean and you do the food.

11. I'm really not happy with your delivery service. I called _____ times last week to arrange an important delivery, but it still hasn't come.

12. The problem with faulty electrical devices, like mobile phones, is that they cost so much to _____, it's cheaper to buy a new one.

69

39. pellere 1

Put the most suitable word in each space. Think about the part of speech required in each space. Make sure you use the correct form.

compel, compulsion, compulsive, peal, propel, propeller, propulsion, pulsar, pulsate, pulse, push, repulse

1. It was only after Jim lost all his money playing roulette that he realised that he had become a _____ gambler. He just couldn't resist having a bet.

2. Scientists are studying a new form of rocket _____, which will allow astronauts to travel across space much faster than they can now.

3. The attacking army laid siege to the city for a month, but each time they attacked, the defenders successfully _____ them.

4. As soon as the happy couple arrived outside the church to get married, the wedding bells started to _____ to announce their arrival.

5. As soon as the paramedics arrived, they checked the victim's _____ and found that his heart was still beating. After a few minutes, he was conscious.

6. As the race reached its climax on the last lap, Alan Matthews accelerated and _____ his car past the leader to win his first Grand Prix.

7. As he looked at the dark, scary house, Alex felt a strange _____ to go inside, even though he knew he shouldn't. Slowly, he opened the door.

8. Sometimes I found the coursework and exam revision so difficult I had to keep _____ myself to get it done, but I'm glad I did in the end.

9. I had a real scare during my flying lesson when one of the _____ on my training plane cut out, but luckily the instructor managed to land safely.

10. The robbers kidnapped the bank manager's family and _____ him to open the bank for them to steal the money.

11. Astronomers have detected radio signals from a new _____, located around a thousand light years from Earth.

12. The game was fantastic, with both sides playing open football. It reached a _____ climax when United scored in the last minute.

40. pellere 2

Put the most suitable word in each space. Think about the part of speech required in each space. Make sure you use the correct form.

appeal, dispel, expel, expulsion, impel, impulse, impulsive, propellant, pushy, repeal, repel, repulsive

1. A week lying on a beach in the sun just doesn't _____ to me as a holiday. I much prefer doing something active, like hiking in the mountains.

2. Whenever I go shopping, I always make a list of things to buy, and buy only those. I never buy things on _____, because I'd spend too much money if I did.

3. Some of the most serious pollutants in the atmosphere are CFCs. These chemicals used to be used as _____ in spray cans.

4. The new government has said it would _____ the law which required all marriages to be performed in a church, and bring in a new one.

5. Jimmy behaved so badly when he was younger that he was _____ from three schools, but his behaviour has really improved now at his new school.

6. Some people say that if you rub lemon juice on your skin before you sleep, it will _____ mosquitoes so that they won't bite you.

7. Here is the weather. Tomorrow will start very misty, but the wind from the south will gradually _____ the mist and it will turn out warm and sunny.

8. When he saw the little girl begging in the street, Arthur felt _____ to do something about it, so he went up and asked her why she was there.

9. The British government today condemned the _____ of three of its diplomats from Russia, saying there was no acceptable reason for it.

10. The largest flower in the world is Rafflesia. It has a smell like rotting meat, which attracts flies, but which people find absolutely _____.

11. I know it's important for parents to encourage their children to do sport or music, but some parents are far too _____ with their kids.

12. Your problem when you play chess is that you're too _____. You have to stop and think a while before you make your move.

41. persona

Put the most suitable word in each space. Think about the part of speech required in each space. Make sure you use the correct form.

depersonalise, impersonal, impersonate, person, persona, personable, personage, personalised, personality, personally, personify, personnel

1. As a chess player, Kuznetsov is one of the best there has ever been, but as a _____, he's not very likeable and rather boring.

2. The police treated us as if we were an annoying distraction, even though we're the victims of the crime. They were so unsympathetic and _____.

3. The company needs someone with a very friendly, outgoing _____, because the successful applicant will be dealing directly with the public.

4. Our captain _____ the spirit of the team. He's athletic, fearless and brave, and never gives up until the end of the game.

5. Do you like my new car? I got it yesterday. It's got all the latest gadgets. I even got a _____ number plate with my name on it for it for £1000.

6. When you arrive for your interview, please go straight to the _____ department on the second floor, where the interview will take place.

7. Did you hear about Peter? He was sacked because he wasn't a real doctor. He was actually _____ a doctor. He fooled everyone in the hospital.

8. Apparently, an important _____ is going to visit the school today. I think it may be the Prime Minister, or maybe even the Queen.

9. A lot of people say that Tommy Craig is a very difficult actor to work with, but when we made a film together, I found him _____ and easy-going.

10. Thelma is a very complicated woman. She tends to put on various different _____ depending on who she's with and how she feels.

11. A lot of people say that Penny and Harry are made for each other, but, _____ speaking, I don't think their relationship will last.

12. These days, organisations often use a number or a code to refer to people and deal with them. I think it _____ people not to use names.

42. placere, placare

Put the most suitable word in each space. Think about the part of speech required in each space. Make sure you use the correct form.

complacent, displease, displeasure, implacable, placebo, placid, plea, plead, pleasant, please, pleasurable, pleasure

1. At the moment the lake is very _____, but when it gets windy and stormy, the water can get quite rough and you can't go out in a boat.
2. Tony was really mean to his wife. Despite all her _____ for him to give her money to help with the children, he always ignored her.
3. You have to be careful with the boss. If you _____ him in any way he can be really ruthless and unforgiving. You might even lose your job.
4. Scientists have shown in many medical trials that a _____ pill can work just as well as real medicine in making people better.
5. Have you looked outside yet? It's a really _____ day. Perhaps we should take the children out for a picnic while the weather stays nice.
6. I told my dad I was really sorry for crashing his car, but he was really angry and completely _____. He said I had to work to pay for the repair bill.
7. It gives me great _____ to present to you on stage tonight the next great singing star of our times, Jenny Porter. Let's here it for Jenny!
8. Last week, I went to a health farm and had a weekend of saunas, massages and beauty treatment. It was such a _____ experience.
9. After the meeting, the President showed his _____ with the press by refusing to make any comments. He just walked straight out of the building.
10. I don't know what more I can do for my husband. I try so hard to _____ him, but nothing I do is good enough. He's never satisfied.
11. I know that the opposition doesn't look very good, but we shouldn't be too _____ and think we'll win, because they could cause us problems.
12. The police have evidence that you were there at the scene of the crime, so the best thing for you is to _____ guilty and get a short sentence.

43. plicare, plectere 1

Put the most suitable word in each space. Think about the part of speech required in each space. Make sure you use the correct form.

appliance, applicable, applicant, application, apply, employ, explicit, exploit, inexplicable, perplex, replicate, triplicate

1. Our shop sells all kinds of household _____, from washing machines and fridges to televisions and hi-fi.

2. I'm really sorry. His behaviour is _____. Usually he's such a quiet and docile dog, so I don't know why he was acting so aggressively towards you.

3. The rule about staying in the school during lunch is only _____ to the younger students, not the older ones. You can go out if you want.

4. We put the job advert in the newspaper only last Monday and we already have over a hundred _____. We need to select some for an interview.

5. If the company gets this new contract, we'll have to _____ over a hundred new workers to fulfil it. It will be great for the local economy.

6. When I first tried to learn Chinese I was so _____ by the writing system that I almost gave up, but I worked hard on it and I can read it well now.

7. I gave Craig _____ instructions about how to install the software, but he didn't listen and as a result it's not working. I couldn't have been clearer.

8. There's a group of people just outside town who are trying to _____ a village from a thousand years ago in exact detail. Do you want to go and see it?

9. After a lifetime spent travelling around the world, Charles Kingston has decided to write a book about all his _____ in the countries he visited.

10. You need to make sure you _____ for university before December to get in next September. You have to fill in the form online.

11. If you don't want to work here any more you have to submit your resignation letter in _____, one copy for you and two for the company.

12. If you want to succeed in life, you have to show far greater _____ in your work. You really don't try hard enough.

44. plicare, plectere 2

Put the most suitable word in each space. Think about the part of speech required in each space. Make sure you use the correct form.

accomplice, complicit, complex, complexion, complicate, duplicate, duplicity, exploitation, implicate, implicit, imply, reduplicate

1. Although Tom did not take part in the bank robbery itself, the police arrested him as he was _____ in the planning of the robbery.
2. Can you believe the level of my boyfriend's _____? He told me he loved me, but all the time he was secretly seeing another woman. I hate him!
3. The government has proposed new laws to stop the _____ of those workers who have to work long hours in poor conditions and for little pay.
4. This is a very _____ court case and the jury won't be able to reach a verdict quickly, so they might have to take a few days to discuss it and decide.
5. I'm afraid I've lost my identity card, but I can get a _____ and bring it here tomorrow, if that's OK.
6. It seems the pickpocket wasn't working alone stealing money on the train and he had at least two _____. The police are looking for them now.
7. When I say that you have to work harder to pass the exam, I don't mean to _____ that you're lazy. I just mean you have a lot of work to do.
8. Look, I know you want me to help you launder the money, but I just can't. I've got a business to run, and I can't be _____ in any sort of criminal activity.
9. I can't believe she's fifty! I mean, look at her _____. She looks so young. How can she keep her skin in such good condition?
10. If you ask someone what they're doing at a specific time in the future, it's _____ in the question that you want to arrange something to do.
11. I'm really not sure when I'll finish work and I don't want to _____ things, so just go ahead to the restaurant without me and I'll come when I can.
12. Look. This is silly. We're just _____ each other's work. Why don't we organise our work so that we don't end up doing the same thing?

45. plicare, plectere 3

Put the most suitable word in each space. Think about the part of speech required in each space. Make sure you use the correct form.

complexity, deploy, display, plait, pleat, pliable, pliant, pliers, plight, ply, replica, reply

1. I know the boss of this organisation and he's very _____. You just offer him a few thousand pounds and he'll do anything for you.

2. My sister always wore her hair tied up in _____ until she was about 18, and then she decided to cut it all off and keep it short.

3. We are going to _____ the new archaeological finds to the public in the museum in the next few weeks, when we've finished cataloguing them.

4. Have you got a pair of _____? This nail is really stuck in the wood and I need to pull it out.

5. John used to _____ his trade as a door-to-door salesman, but nowadays you can get everything on the internet, so he uses that now.

6. I'm afraid there's no _____ from Mr Smith's phone. He must have switched it off. If you like I can try to ring him again in fifteen minutes.

7. Can you iron this dress for me? Be careful to iron the _____ nicely. I don't want any extra creases in it.

8. This type of wood is very _____, so it's ideal for building small boats where the wood has to be bent slightly.

9. The general _____ his army on the high ground so that they would gain a material advantage over the enemy before the battle.

10. When we found the survivors on the boat, they were in an absolutely terrible _____. They were hungry, cold and thirsty, and had no shelter.

11. The original statue is being restored, so the museum has decided to put a _____ on display until the original is ready to be put back.

12. As you move up the levels of this computer game, the action increases in _____, so that by the end it's almost impossible to win.

46. porta, portare, portus 1

Put the most suitable word in each space. Think about the part of speech required in each space. Make sure you use the correct form.

deport, disport, export, import, importune, purport, report, sporting (2), support, supporter, transport

1. The biggest problem for most parents today is that they have to work so hard to earn enough money to _____ their families.

2. During the presidential election campaign, Jim Shrub lost many _____ when he admitted that he had lied about taking drugs when he was at university.

3. In the football game, Toni kicked the ball out when he saw the goalkeeper was badly injured. It was a very _____ act, as he could have scored.

4. The police have arrested fifty illegal immigrants, who were working without visas or work permits. They will be _____ back to their countries.

5. When you have finished creating your picture on the computer, you should then _____ it in GIF format so that you can put it on your website.

6. In the 19th century rich people would regularly _____ themselves in leisure activities, such as hunting, shooting and fishing.

7. If you continue to behave in this unacceptable way, I'll have no choice but to _____ you to the headmaster and you'll be in serious trouble.

8. The government has to understand that the railway is the most economical and environmentally friendly way to _____ goods around the country.

9. The historian, Geoffrey Hunter, has written a controversial new book which _____ to tell the true story of the modern royal family.

10. The Daily News has published a story about the actor, Julian Lewis, partying in a nightclub without his wife, while _____ young women for sex.

11. The problem with this computer programme is you can't _____ files which have been saved in another format. You have to convert them first.

12. When we all arrived at work today, there was Damian, _____ a new beard that he had grown over the holiday. I really don't think it suits him.

47. porta, portare, portus 2

Put the most suitable word in each space. Think about the part of speech required in each space. Make sure you use the correct form.

importance, opportunity, port, portable, portage, portal, porter, portfolio, portico, portly, rapport

1. It's typical, isn't it? I arrive at the station with lots of heavy bags and I can't find a _____ to help me when I need one.

2. You've been offered a job in New York? What a fantastic _____! You've always wanted to live and work there, so if I were you, I'd accept it right away.

3. Did you see Rolf at the party last night? He looked really _____. The last time I saw him five years ago he looked really slim and fit, not fat at all.

4. Although this was the first meeting between the two presidents, they clearly established a _____, smiling and laughing together in public.

5. The political scandal was a matter of such great _____ that the Prime Minister decided to cancel his official trip to China in order to deal with it personally.

6. If you want to invest your money, you shouldn't put it in just one company, but put together a _____ of different investments in various companies.

7. At the back of the computer there are various _____ which you can use to connect printers, disk drives and other equipment.

8. If we look here at the entrance to the building, we can see the marvellous Italian style _____, which was built in the 16th century.

9. I found a really good internet _____ yesterday. It gives you email and plenty of space to set up a website, show off your photos and a lot more.

10. In the old days before the canal was built, sailors had to sail up one river and pull their boats along a _____ way to get to the other river.

11. I've bought a new _____ bicycle. I ride to the station, pack it away in its case, take the train into town, unpack it and cycle to work.

48. potis

Put the most suitable word in each space. Think about the part of speech required in each space. Make sure you use the correct form.

dispossess, empower, impotence, posse, possess, possessive, possible, potent, potential, power, prepossess, repossess

1. Jim seemed fine when we started dating, but since we've been married he's became so jealous and _____ that he won't let me out of his sight.

2. Medical scientists are worried that _____ among men is increasing, with many couples finding it difficult to conceive and have children.

3. I'm really worried that if we don't make our next mortgage payment, the bank is going to _____ our house and leave us homeless.

4. There are three _____ outcomes to this situation: the company downsizes, it goes bankrupt, or I sell it. I'd prefer the third, but we must decide.

5. The new reforms to the electoral system will_____ the voters far more and give them a far greater chance to influence government policy.

6. I've been watching Joe in his athletics training and I really think, if he carries on improving, he's a _____ world champion. He can be the best.

7. The sheriff managed to get together a _____ of deputies and together they set out to find and arrest the bank robbers.

8. Although Jim Tree is the President, the real _____ lies in the hands of the Vice-President, Rick Chantry, who influences everything the President decides.

9. I don't know what _____ you to drive the car without a licence or insurance, but you're lucky the police didn't stop you and arrest you.

10. Be careful if you drink the local fire water. It's so _____ you could easily get really drunk on just a couple of glasses.

11. The club shouldn't buy that player. He doesn't _____ the speed and skill required to play in a top football team. He'll be a waste of money.

12. The problem with the collapse of this bank is that thousands of people have been _____. All their savings have disappeared without trace.

49. praehendere 1

Put the most suitable word in each space. Think about the part of speech required in each space. Make sure you use the correct form.

apprehend, apprehension, apprehensive, apprentice, apprise, comprehend, comprehensive, comprise, enterprise, entrepreneur, impresario, surprise

1. When you go up on stage, you mustn't show any _____ or signs of nervousness. Just be confident of your singing ability and you'll be fine.

2. At first, Lee couldn't quite _____ what he had done, but it was true. He had won the Olympic 100 metres final. At last, the gold medal was his.

3. The theatre _____, Jim Lowther, has said he is going to produce a new version of the musical, Les Miserables, with a cast of unknown teenagers.

4. As you can see, this apartment _____ four bedrooms, a living room, a kitchen, a dining room and a study, with a large balcony outside.

5. After two years as an _____ jockey, Laurie Mason has won 100 races in his first season as a professional rider, which puts him third in the championship.

6. The education minister is planning _____ reforms to the school selection system to make it easier for parents to choose the right school.

7. We have decided to set up a joint _____ between our two companies to produce a new generation of more powerful computer chips.

8. When we meet next month, I'll _____ you of any changes that have been made in college policy during your absence. Have a good trip!

9. I hadn't seen my brother for five years, but when I got home last night, I opened the door and there he was. What a lovely _____ it was!

10. After the fall of communism, the situation was perfect for any smart, budding _____ to set up a business and make a lot of money.

11. My daughter wants to go on holiday with friends. I know she's sixteen and very sensible, but I'm a bit _____ about it. What do you think?

12. Police have _____ three men who, they believe, tried to break into Buckingham Palace to kidnap the Queen last night.

80

50. praehendere 2

Put the most suitable word in each space. Think about the part of speech required in each space. Make sure you use the correct form.

depredation, prehensile, predator, predatory, prey, prise, prison, reprehend,
reprehensible, reprieve, reprisal, reprise

1. Last night government soldiers went around the capital shooting people indiscriminately in _____ for the attempt on the president's life.

2. Only monkeys in South America have _____ tails, which enable them to hang from trees. African and Indian monkeys are not able to do this.

3. When the teacher found out that the boys had been playing with the fire extinguisher, he _____ them severely in front of the whole class.

4. My grandfather fell into a life of crime from a young age and spent half his life in _____. He finally managed to change and has been out for years.

5. The judge was going to send Ross to jail for his part in the bank fraud, but granted him a _____ as long as he did not commit another crime.

6. When I checked the window, I found scratches and dents on the frame. Someone had tried to _____ it open while I was out, so I called the police.

7. The monkeys spend most of the day looking for food on the savannah, but they run for cover in a tree when a _____, like an eagle, comes.

8. I know that the accident was your fault, but the behaviour of the other driver was completely _____. He had no right to hit you.

9. Originally, there were thousands of dodos on Mauritius, but these birds became extinct as a result of _____ by cats and rats after humans arrived.

10. As the football teams come out onto the field, Milan's manager will be hoping for a _____ of last year's performance, when they won 5-0.

11. Although cats were domesticated thousands of years ago, they still retain their natural _____ instincts and hunt rats, mice and birds.

12. The eagle circled high in the sky, but as soon as it saw its _____, a small deer, far below, it swooped down and caught it in its talons.

51. premere 1

All these words are verbs. Put the most suitable verb in each space. Make sure you use the correct form and tense where necessary.

compress, depress, depressurise, express, impress, oppress, pressurise, print, repress, reprimand, reprint, suppress

1. I didn't want to go to medical school, but my parents _____ me so much that I felt I had to go to please them. In the event, I gave up after a year.

2. I'm sorry. We can't get that book at this shop at the moment. The publishers are going to _____ it soon if you want to place an order for order it.

3. During the election campaign, the government party tried to _____ a story about their candidate's extra-marital love affair, but a reporter found out.

4. Elaine's big problem is that she finds it very difficult to _____ her true feelings to the people that she loves, and they think she doesn't care.

5. You've researched so much information on this subject that you have to find a way to _____ it into just a thousand word essay.

6. I really don't like living here in winter. It's cold and wet and there's nothing to do. It _____ me so much that I really want to move away.

7. If I write a letter to the newspaper, do you think they'll _____ it? It would be really nice to see my name on the letters page.

8. Remember. When you do the audition for a part in the new play, don't try hard to _____ the producer. Just be your natural self, and you'll be fine.

9. In ancient Rome, the slaves were so _____ by their masters that they revolted, fought a war and almost won it under their leader, Spartacus.

10. After you finish your dive to the sea bed, make sure you come to the surface really slowly to allow the air in your body to _____.

11. My meeting with the office manager wasn't as bad as I thought. I was officially _____ for being late six times this month, but I won't lose my job.

12. After three days of student demonstrations, the government finally lost patience, and used to army to _____ the protests and apprehend the leaders.

52. premere 2

Put the most suitable word in each space. Think about the part of speech required in each space. Make sure you use the correct form.

depression, express, expression, expressive, impression, impressive, imprint, oppressive, press, pressing, pressure, repressive

1. I think Peter Johnson is the best person for the job. His experience and qualifications are very _____. I can't see anyone better.

2. Whatever you do, don't talk to the _____. If the newspapers find out anything about this scandal, it could seriously affect your political career.

3. At first when Sara saw me she had a very puzzled _____ on her face, but then she remembered me and cried with joy, "Daddy! You're back!"

4. Look! I've got enough _____ on me at the moment, with my final exams coming up and all the revision, so I don't need any more of it now.

5. When I was living in Indonesia, I found the constant heat and humidity really _____. It was difficult to find the energy to do anything.

6. After my wife left me and took the children, I lost my job and then my house. I just went into a deep _____ for two years. It was terrible.

7. You have to help me. This is a really _____ problem and it can't wait until next week. I have to sort it out now, or I might lose my house.

8. I gave you _____ instructions not to let anybody use my office in my absence, but you didn't listen. Now my computer's broken and I can't use it.

9. At the audition, all of the performers could sing and dance, but Jane was the only one who made a real _____ on me. She was great.

10. Why do you have to push down so hard with the pen? Just look at the _____ of your writing that you've made in the wood on the table.

11. Twenty years ago, this country was ruled by a very _____ regime that didn't allow any opposition, but now we're free and we have a democracy.

12. Although Jimmy's only two years old, he's very _____ already. He can tell us exactly what he wants very clearly and easily.

53. pungere 1

Put the most suitable word in each space. Think about the part of speech required in each space. Make sure you use the correct form.

appoint, compunction, disappoint, expunge, poignant, point (v), pounce, punch, punchy, pungent

1. In the film, Titanic, when the heroine finally realises her lover is dead and she lets him go in the water, it was such a _____ moment that I cried.

2. I had no _____ about leaving my husband when I found out about his love affair with his secretary at work, even though he begged me to forgive him.

3. Before you start the exam, I just want to _____ out a few things for you to remember, in particular the exam regulations.

4. After it was found that Tom Kelly had lied about his qualifications and experience, his name was _____ from the shortlist for the management position.

5. I never really wanted to become a doctor. I did it mainly so I wouldn't _____ my parents, who desperately wanted to me to study medicine.

6. Although Christina May lost her tennis match against the reigning champion, her performance was so brave and _____ that the crowd loved her.

7. We watched as the cat crawled slowly and silently towards the mouse; then it suddenly _____ on the mouse and caught it in its claws.

8. We have interviewed five candidates for the vacant manager's post, and we expect to _____ a new manager by the end of the week.

9. I dropped some perfumed oil in the bathwater and within a few minutes its sweet, _____ scent filled the bathroom. It really helped me relax.

10. As the Prime Minister walked into the meeting, someone threw and egg at him, so he turned round and _____ him! I couldn't believe my eyes!

54. pungere 2

Put the most suitable word in each space. Think about the part of speech required in each space. Make sure you use the correct form.

point (n), point-blank, pointed, pointless, punctilious, punctual, punctuality, punctuate, punctuation, puncture

1. I'm sorry I'm late. I left home early, but the car had a _____ on the way, and I had to change the tyre by myself. That's why I'm so dirty.

2. As the President waved to the crowds, a man with a gun stepped in front of him and shot him _____ in the chest from less than a metre away.

3. My Latin teacher at school was the most _____ person I've ever known. All the work we did in class had to be completed correctly and in detail.

4. My aunt's whole life was _____ by tragic events, like the death of her first child, her husband's suicide, the fire in her house and, finally, her cancer.

5. Listen. It's completely _____ trying to persuade Tony to come out with us. He just doesn't want to. Let's just leave him and go out by ourselves.

6. The teacher said that my spelling and handwriting were good, but the main problem is my _____. I need to how to use commas and full stops correctly.

7. Most of the students in my class come on time, but Hans has a real problem with _____. I think he's arrived at school on time only three times.

8. During the discussion about the school's financial situation, Jim made the _____ that there's very little money available to buy new books.

9. In his latest book about American society, Laurie Barker makes some very relevant and _____ comments on the current political situation.

10. The best thing about the railway system in this country is that there are frequent trains and they're always _____. I've never seen one come late.

55. regere 1

Put the most suitable word in each space. Think about the part of speech required in each space. Make sure you use the correct form.

realm, regal, regalia, regent, regime, regimen, regiment, region, reign, royal, royalty, rule

1. What really annoys me about the president's family is that they all behave as if they were _____, when really they're just ordinary people like us.

2. At 64 years, Queen Victoria's _____, from 1837 to 1901, is the longest of any monarch in British history.

3. I'm really worried about my brother's future. The army has told us that his whole _____ is going to be sent to fight in a war zone.

4. Over the last fifty years, the climate in this _____ has become a lot drier, resulting in the gradual expansion of the Sahara desert.

5. When the king died, his son was only seven, so the dead king's brother acted as prince _____ until the young king grew up.

6. At the ceremony the old soldiers were all dressed in their uniforms and decorated with their _____. They all looked very proud and smart.

7. The best way for you to lose weight is to make some basic changes to your normal eating _____, such as cutting out snacks between meals.

8. The little prince looked so _____, dressed up in his fine clothes and with the crown on his head.

9. Tara claims she has _____ blood, because her great grandmother was a cousin of the king, but I don't believe her.

10. By the 2nd century CE, most of Europe, North Africa and the Eastern Mediterranean had fallen under Roman _____ as the empire spread.

11. In 1989, all the communist _____ in Eastern Europe fell from power and democracy was restored.

12. The king decided that he wanted to find out how many people lived in his _____, so he ordered his officials to conduct a census.

56. regere 2

Put the most suitable word in each space. Think about the part of speech required in each space. Make sure you use the correct form.

adroit, derail, erect, irregular, rail, rectangular, rectify, rectitude, rector, regular, regulate, regulation

1. My father was a model of _____. I never heard him swear or say any bad things about anyone. He was always polite and honest.
2. The mountain path used to be quite dangerous, but that was before they put in a _____ on the side to make sure you don't fall down.
3. We apologise for the loss of your television service. Our engineers are working hard to _____ the situation as soon as possible.
4. Every college at this university has a _____, whose job is to look after the welfare of the students and make sure the college runs well.
5. Although many people doubted the new Prime Minister's ability, he was very _____ in dealing successfully with his first crisis after the election.
6. The doctor told me that I need to cut down on fatty foods and take more _____ exercise, like running or doing aerobics every day.
7. Most sports fields are _____ in shape, but some games, like cricket, are played on oval fields.
8. The college _____ clearly states that smoking is only allowed in the area at the back of the building, so you have to go out there to smoke.
9. The city council has decided to _____ a statue of the city's founder, Josiah Robinson, in the centre of the city square.
10. We are getting reports that a commuter train has _____ just outside Leeds. Emergency services are at the scene and the line is closed.
11. At the moment there are no restrictions on people who call themselves financial advisers. Anyone can do it. The government needs to _____ them.
12. The accountant found a number of _____ payments in the company accounts. He wants to know what they are and who they were for.

57. regere 3

Put the most suitable word in each space. Think about the part of speech required in each space. Make sure you use the correct form.

address, correct, direct, directory, dress, incorrigible, insurgent, insurrection, redress resurgent, resurrect, surge

1. As soon as the gates of the stadium opened for the big game, the excited crowd _____ forward, trying to be the first to get inside.

2. Every time we go out, you have to behave badly and embarrass me, even though I tell you not to. You're absolutely _____! You never do the right thing.

3. It is customary for the Queen to give her annual television _____ to the nation at 3.00 on Christmas Day.

4. I've decided to put our business details into a new local online business _____, so that customers can find us much more easily.

5. There's no formal _____ code at that new nightclub in town, but they don't let you in if you're wearing jeans and trainers.

6. The latest reports say that soldiers fought a fierce battle with anti-government _____ in the south of the country, with casualties on both sides.

7. I don't think I'll be able to get away from work soon. The students did their mock tests today and I have to _____ them by tomorrow morning.

8. Last year the team didn't win any of their last ten games, but under the new manager, they have been _____ and haven't lost a single game.

9. These days the rich are getting richer and the poor are getting poorer, so we need to raise taxes and use the money to _____ the balance.

10. Do you remember that children's programme, Down On The Farm, when we were kids? Well, the new TV company is going to _____ it.

11. Before we start the meeting, I just want to remind you that if you have any questions or comments, you need to _____ them to the chair.

12. The government says the army has finally put down the _____, which has been running for ten years in the north of the country.

58. sacer, sancire

Put the most suitable word in each space. Think about the part of speech required in each space. Make sure you use the correct form.

consecrate, desecrate, execrable, sacred, sacrifice, sacrilege, sacrosanct, saint, sanctimonious, sanction, sanctity, sanctuary

1. My parents were very poor and made a lot of _____ to save money for me to go to university, so it's my duty to take care of them now that they're old.

2. I can't stand that man! He's so _____! He thinks he alone knows what's good and right, and he just looks down on everyone else.

3. When I got home I found that someone had broken in and looked through all my person belongings. It felt like my home had been _____.

4. When Jimmy Taylor came back to play for his home town football team, he was so popular and well-loved that the people treated him like a _____.

5. I went to see Simon Steinberg's latest film yesterday. I thought his first two were good, but this one's really _____. It's the worst film he's made.

6. When I saw how much the animals were badly treated and forced to perform, I decided to create a _____ for them to live freely and without fear.

7. Many couples have a wedding in church to _____ their marriage, but they still have to sign the marriage register to make it legal.

8. This stadium was built to play rugby, and many rugby supporters feel that playing soccer games there would somehow violate its _____.

9. When Keith Latimer wanted to stand as the official candidate for mayor, the party refused to _____ it, so he stood as an independent and won.

10. I'm sorry, but my Saturday afternoons are _____. That's when I go to watch the football and I'm not giving it up for work, or anything else.

11. Most religions of the world have a _____ book with all their teachings, like the Bible, the Koran or the Bhagavad-Gita.

12. A lot of men regarded it as _____ to allow women to join their men's club, or to even be allowed into the front doors.

59. sedere 1

Put the most suitable word in each space. Think about the part of speech required in each space. Make sure you use the correct form.

assess, assiduous, besiege, dissident, insidious, obsession, preside, president, reside, residue, subside, supersede

1.   The floods _____ after completely covering the town for a week. Only then could the local people see how bad the damage was.

2.   Geoff is one of the most _____ workers we have in the company. He always takes time over his projects and completes them accurately and carefully.

3.   After the grape juice has turned into wine, you have to bottle it. Don't let any of the _____ from the bottom of the barrel get into the bottles.

4.   As soon as the photographers found out the identity of the prince's new girlfriend, dozens of them _____ her house to get a picture.

5.   Ever since I first picked up a book when I was a boy, I've loved reading. I always carry a book with me. It's a real _____. I can't be without one.

6.   The police arrested many of the anti-government _____, who had been protesting against the new law banning gatherings of more than six people.

7.   This government has _____ over the biggest period of economic growth in this country over the last fifty years.

8.   The Queen only _____ here in the summer, when the flag flies over the palace.

9.   At the end of the course you will be _____ both on the work that you have done through the year and on a final exam, which you will do in June.

10.   I'm afraid we've had to make some changes to the timetable again. Here's the new one. It _____ all the previous ones, so throw those away.

11.   It gives me great pleasure to announce that Gerald Wiseman has been elected as the new _____ of our film society.

12.   The government has to do something about the growth of armed criminal gangs and their _____ and harmful effect on our society.

60. sedere 2

Put the most suitable word in each space. Think about the part of speech required in each space. Make sure you use the correct form.

obsessed, resident, residual, séance, sedate, sedentary, sediment, session, siege, size, subsidiary, subsidy

1. Every year thousands of tonnes of soil and mud from the desert are carried down the River Nile and deposited in the delta as _____.

2. If you can't get to the training _____ at the sports centre today, don't worry. There's going to be an extra one tomorrow afternoon at 3.00.

3. As rice is the most important part of people's diet in this country, the government provides heavy _____ to keep the price low enough for everyone.

4. There's going to be a meeting tomorrow at the town hall for all the _____ of this area to debate the proposed traffic-calming scheme.

5. Doctors are very worried about children's health these days. Their _____ lifestyle means that few of them get enough exercise.

6. Although the trade union's members are prepared to accept the pay agreement, there's still _____ anger about the management's negative tactics.

7. I attended a _____ last night. The other people said that we managed to call up a spirit to talk to, but I don't think that we did really. It was just a bit of fun.

8. The business is doing so well we're opening up five new _____ offices in America and Europe to expand the market for our products.

9. Jane had to call the police about her neighbour yesterday. He's become so _____ with her that he keeps following her around everywhere.

10. One thing that surprised me when I saw the Taj Mahal for the first time was the sheer _____ of the building. It's absolutely massive.

11. When the ambulance brought Hilary to hospital after the accident, she was so distressed that doctors had to _____ her before they operated.

12. According to Homer's Iliad, the Greeks laid _____ to Troy for ten years before they managed to enter the city in the wooden horse and sack it.

61. sentire 1

All these words are adjectives. Put the most suitable adjective in each space.

insensible, insensitive, sensational, senseless, sensible, sensitive, sensory, sensual, sensuous, sententious, sentient, sentimental

1. I was really enjoying the party, until I saw my husband lying drunk on the floor, totally _____ to the music and dancing going on around him.
2. I just turned on the news and heard that the President has been arrested for fraud. Can you believe it? It's absolutely _____ news!
3. A lot of people oppose animal experiments on the grounds that it's cruel to carry them out on _____ beings, especially dogs and monkeys.
4. For me there's nothing more delightful and _____ than a hot herbal bath, followed by a massage and a candlelit dinner with my husband.
5. How can you be so _____? You knew that Jane's cat died yesterday. Why on earth did you have to make a joke about it and make her cry?
6. Police are investigating a robbery at the bank, when the robber shot a cashier dead after taking the money. It was a totally _____ and needless act.
7. I hate it when I hear the Prime Minister speaking. He talks in such an arrogant and _____ way, as if he were morally superior to everyone else.
8. I think people are far more _____ about not drinking and driving these days, and that's why driving offences and accidents are going down.
9. At the end of a party I love dancing to slow, _____ music with my boyfriend. It really gets us in the mood for love.
10. I've got a new smoke detector, but it's far too _____. Any tiny amount of smoke makes it start buzzing. It's driving me mad.
11. I hate the way _____ films try so hard to make the audience feel really sad and cry. It's so false. Give me good, hard action films any time.
12. I love visiting open markets because they have such _____ delights, like the sights and sounds of the people, and the smell and taste of the food.

62. sentire 2

Put the most suitable word in each space. Think about the part of speech required in each space. Make sure you use the correct form.

assent, consensus, consent, dissent, nonsense, resent, sensation, sense, sensitize, sensor, sentence, sentiment

1. Whoever told you that I failed my driving test? Whatever they said, don't believe a word of it. It's complete _____. I passed!

2. Despite the lack of agreement about who should be the next England football team manager, there was a _____ that he should be English.

3. You know what your problem is. You've always _____ the fact that I went to university and you didn't. You really need to let it go and grow up.

4. The important thing to remember when you're composing a grammatical _____ is that it always has to have a subject and a verb.

5. I woke up in hospital three days after the accident. I tried to sit up, but then I realised I had no _____ in my legs. I had broken my spine.

6. One of the most amazing things about sharks is that they can detect electrical activity from other fish in the water through _____ in their skin.

7. When Tony finally realised the level of _____ with his management style among the staff, he decided the only thing to do was to resign.

8. As soon as I arrived at my grandmother's and found the door wide open, I _____ that something serious had happened to her.

9. The students said that you were the best teacher they've ever had, and I agree entirely with that _____. You've been absolutely marvellous.

10. The aim of this charity campaign is to _____ us all to the problems of poor people in other countries, so that we understand the need to donate more.

11. Traditionally, when the newly elected British Prime Minister visits the Queen to ask permission to form a government, she must _____ to it.

12. I'm really angry with the newspaper editor for using my picture in the paper. He never asked me and I certainly never _____ to it.

93

63. signum

Put the most suitable word in each space. Think about the part of speech required in each space. Make sure you use the correct form.

assign, consign, design, insignia, resign, seal, sign, signal, signatory, signature, significant, signify

1. The test explosion of the first atomic bomb in the American desert _____ the dawn of the nuclear age and a new global threat.

2. During the driving test, it's really important to remember to check your mirror and give the correct _____ every time before you turn.

3. We felt that we needed a new image, so we decided to _____ this new logo to put on the company's paperwork and products. What do you think?

4. I've had enough of this job. I can't stand working here any more, so I've decided to _____ with immediate effect. I'm going to find a new job.

5. After the popular revolutions in Eastern Europe in 1989, all the communist regimes fell and communism was eventually _____ to history.

6. I've got some great news! The company is going to open a new office in Paris, and I've been _____ there as the new manager. I'm so excited!

7. Look at this shield. It carries the royal _____ of the first Norman king of England, William the Conqueror. It must be worth millions!

8. Since we adopted the new teaching methods we have noticed a _____ improvement in the students' performance. They're really motivated to learn.

9. Before envelopes were used for letters, rich people would use a personal wax _____ to close the letter and to show that they sent it.

10. It is really not possible for this government, as a _____ to the agreement on nuclear disarmament, to carry out new atomic bomb tests.

11. OK. I've checked the form and we have all your details. Now all we need is your _____ here at the bottom and it's completed.

12. The recent fall in the crime figures is a clear _____ that the government policies to reduce crime are finally starting to work.

64. similis

Put the most suitable word in each space. Think about the part of speech required in each space. Make sure you use the correct form.

assimilate, dissemble, dissimilar, resemblance, resemble, semblance, similar, similarly, simile, simulate, simulation, simultaneously

1. Though John and James are twins, they actually look quite _____, to the extent that people don't even think they're brothers.

2. A very popular way of describing things is to use a _____, for example, "as big as a house", or "as cold as ice".

3. On his last day of work at the office, Jim told us that he was happy to leave, but there was a _____ of regret in his voice as he spoke.

4. It is important for people who settle in this country to _____ into the society and adopt local customs, while retaining their own cultural identities.

5. As we sat, drank tea and chatted to the guests, George tried to _____ his true feelings with a pleasant smile on his face, but I knew he hated being there.

6. I laughed so much when I saw my husband coming in from the snow, dressed in a big fur coat and fur hat. He really _____ a big brown bear.

7. One of the biggest problems in football today is _____. Too many players pretend to be fouled or injured, when there's really nothing wrong.

8. I wouldn't buy any clothes here. They're far too expensive. You can get _____ ones for half the price at another shop not far from here.

9. In the film "Substitute", the president is killed, so they force Tom, a taxi driver, to act the president because of his extremely close _____ to him.

10. "Fighting Fists" is a really realistic film. Even though I knew that they were only _____ boxing, it really looked like they were doing the real thing.

11. Police said that the terrorists had set the bombs in the cars to explode _____, exactly at 8.30, at the height of the morning rush hour.

12. I'm afraid the library will be closed next week for major repairs, _____ the following week, though it should open after that.

65. singulus, simplex, simul

Put the most suitable word in each space. Think about the part of speech required in each space. Make sure you use the correct form.

assemble, assembly, disassemble, ensemble, simple, simpleton, simplicity, simplify, simplistic, simply, single, singular

1. The problem looks very complex on the surface, but in reality it's very

    _____. You have to look at it in a different way to see the answer.

2. I'm getting together with some other musicians to form a classical music

    _____. We're going to play concerts in the park in summer.

3. All the car parts are made in China and shipped in each month. The cars

    themselves are _____ in the factory here and sent out to the

    showrooms.

4. What I love about the design of our new logo is its _____. Far too

    many companies go for a complex, confusing design, but this is easy on the eye.

5. People used to think that Jack Harris was a bit of a _____, but in

    winning the election he's proved himself a clever and skilful politician.

6. In our library we have all the original classics, but we also have them in

    _____ form, so that lower level students can read and enjoy them.

7. When I was at school we used to have weekly _____ for the whole

    school in the hall every Friday, but my son's school doesn't have them at all.

8. I'm really upset. I've done the lottery every week for the past few years, but on

    the _____ occasion that I don't do it, all my numbers come up.

9. You've got a very _____ view of the world if you think everyone is

    either good or bad. Things are much more complicated than you think.

10. There was a serious problem with the car and I had to _____ the

    engine to find it, but I've repaired it and put everything back together again.

11. I would pay a lot of money to have the _____ pleasure of staying

    in a luxury hotel for just one night in my life.

12. Our holiday was _____ wonderful! The hotel was luxurious, the

    food was delicious, the sea was warm and the weather was lovely.

66. solvere

Put the most suitable word in each space. Think about the part of speech required in each space. Make sure you use the correct form.

absolute, absolve, dissolute, dissolve, resolute, resolution, resolve, soluble, solution (2), solve, solvent

1. If you put oil in water it will just float on the surface and not mix with the water, since oil is not _____ in water.

2. Although I was the car driver in the accident, the police _____ from any blame for it, as I was driving carefully and correctly.

3. The Marquis de Sade led a totally _____ life of drinking, sex and violence, and spent the last years of his life in prison.

4. After you finish painting every day, make sure that you wash out your brushes in a _____ like turpentine, or they will become too stiff to use again.

5. In the Soviet Union, the communist regime held _____ control over political activity and thought. Nobody could succeed if they were not in the party.

6. Although the problems of climate change are extremely complex, there is no reason why we can't find _____ to them if the will to do so is there.

7. I always try to do the crossword in the Sunday newspaper, but I've never managed to _____ all the clues because it's so difficult.

8. In difficult times, leaders have to be _____, stick to their principles and carry their policies through to completion, regardless of what people say.

9. If you have indigestion after you eat, put two teaspoons of this powder into water, wait for it to _____ completely and then drink it.

10. Digital pictures used to have very poor _____ and come out blurred, but the latest digital cameras take pictures which are almost as good as film.

11. The best way to remove stains from your clothes is to soak them overnight in a _____ of soap powder and water.

12. My wife and I worked really hard to _____ the problems in our marriage, but in the end they proved too difficult and we decided to separate.

67. specere 1

Put the most suitable word in each space. Think about the part of speech required in each space. Make sure you use the correct form.

spec, spectacle, spectacular, spectator, spectral, spectre, spectrum, speculate, speculative, speculator

1. It's very difficult to _____ about the company's future, because things are so uncertain, but at the moment business is going quite well.

2. If you ask people in this country about their ideas on politics, you'll find a whole _____ of opinion from the far left to the far right.

3. It's often difficult for ex-criminals to find work, because they always have the _____ of their previous criminal lives hanging over them.

4. There was a _____ accident in the Formula 1 Grand Prix race this afternoon, when four cars crashed on the final bend. Luckily, no one was hurt.

5. As I entered the old house, it was in total darkness, but then I saw a strange figure hovering at the top of the stairs, with a _____ glow all around it.

6. I've got a new job. Last month I sent out my CV on _____ to a lot of colleges and schools in case they had work, and one of them phoned me up.

7. While you're in Brazil, you really should go and see the carnival. It's one of the most amazing and exciting _____ in the world.

8. This is the biggest stadium in the country. When it's full it holds over 90,000 _____, and we expect it to be full tonight.

9. The money markets are often unsettled by currency _____, who try to sell currencies which they think going to lose their value in the near future.

10. Any talk in the newspapers of a change of government at this moment is pure _____. The Prime Minister has no intention of calling an election.

68. specere 2 - species

Put the most suitable word in each space. Think about the part of speech required in each space. Make sure you use the correct form.

especially, special, specialise, specialism, speciality, specially, species, specific, specify, specification, specimen, specious

1. Our expedition to the Amazon was very successful. We collected hundreds of insect _____, some of which are completely new to science.
2. Thank you all very much for coming to our wedding. This has been a really _____ day, one for us to remember all our lives.
3. It's a completely _____ argument for governments to promise tax cuts, because they have to find the money in some other way, but they never say how.
4. Remember, when you make your order for a sofa, you must _____ what kind of material you want on it: leather, cotton or velvet.
5. In the first year at university, you study three subjects, but then you need to choose one to _____ in, with one of the others as a minor subject.
6. Sometimes living in this city gets so frustrating, _____ when the trains aren't working properly, or there's too much traffic in the streets.
7. This computer is the latest model, with a really large memory and hard disk. All the _____ are listed on this information sheet.
8. This restaurant is one of the best in town. The _____ of the chef is roast duck with orange and onion sauce. It's really, very good.
9. It's so expensive to send your children to university nowadays that I've opened an account _____ to save money for my son to go in five years.
10. I gave you _____ instructions not to let anyone in my office while I was out. Why didn't you do what I told you? Now my laptop is missing.
11. At first we thought that the birds on this island were the same as those on the other mainland, but actually, they're a separate _____.
12. One of the lecturers on the university physics course is Professor Jones. His _____ is quantum mechanics.

69. specere 3

Put the most suitable word in each space. Think about the part of speech required in each space. Make sure you use the correct form.

aspect, despicable, despise, despite, expect, expectant, expectation, introspection, perspective, perspicacious, respite, spite

1. My father's been looking after my sick mother all year, so I'm going to take over for a week and give him some _____ and the chance for a holiday.

2. Inspector Holmes is the most _____ police officer in the force. He notices things at a crime scene that no one else does.

3. How can you even think of inviting Joanna to our wedding anniversary party? She was the one who tried to break us up. I really _____ her.

4. My son got three straight 'A's in his exam results, which was well beyond our _____. We had thought he would get 'B's at best.

5. We have to look carefully at every _____ of this problem if we are going to deal with it successfully and find a workable solution.

6. I think Sandra destroyed Julie's painting just out of _____, because the art teacher said that Julie's drawing was better than hers. It's a nasty thing to do.

7. After our poor performance in our last game, there was a great deal of thought and _____ as we tried to work out what went wrong.

8. You should give up you seat on the bus to disabled people, old people and _____ mothers, because they're the ones who need it most.

9. In the end I decided not to take the job in America, _____ the fantastic pay and excellent conditions. It'll be too hard to leave my family behind.

10. The teacher said that three boys hit my son, broke his glasses and took all his money. It can't believe they could do something so _____.

11. I know the results of our first three games have been good, but let's keep things in _____. We've still got a long way to go and a lot to do.

12. I've worked in a lot of different countries, but this is the first time I've worked in China, so it's difficult to know what to _____.

70. specere 4

Put the most suitable word in each space. Think about the part of speech required in each space. Make sure you use the correct form.

conspicuous, disrespectful, inspect, prospect, prospective, prospectus, respect, respectable, respectively, retrospect, suspect, suspicious

1. We've chosen Simon Simpson as the _____ candidate for our party in the election next month. I believe he's the best candidate we've got.

2. It wasn't difficult to pick the bird out against the green background of the trees. It was so _____ with its bright red plumage.

3. Don't forget that someone is coming tomorrow to _____ the school, so make sure you're here on time with all your work in your folders.

4. If you look at the video you can see that man standing outside the bank just before the robbery. I think he looks very _____. Why is he there?

5. With the economy growing steadily, a very low rate of unemployment and a highly educated workforce, the country's economic _____ are excellent.

6. When Alan came in, he saw my parents in the living room, but he just walked past without saying a word. It was so _____. I'm so angry with him.

7. My daughter brought her boyfriend home to meet us yesterday. He seems very nice and polite, and he's from a very _____ family.

8. If you want to see what courses the university is going to offer next year, you can look in our _____, which comes out next month.

9. In some countries, young people still show a lot of _____ to older people, but it seems they don't do it any more in this country.

10. Have you heard about Mr Smith, our neighbour? He's been arrested as a _____ in that recent murder case. I can't believe it.

11. I left university after the second year, but in _____ I should have stayed on and completed it. I would have got a better job if I had.

12. The first three children in the photography competition were given a computer, a camera and an MP3 player _____.

71. stare 1

Put the most suitable word in each space. Think about the part of speech required in each space. Make sure you use the correct form.

stable, stage, staid, state, statement, stationary, statistics, statue, stature, status, statute, stay

1. In ancient Greece the Athenians made a huge marble _____ of the goddess Athena and placed it in front of the Parthenon.
2. When you're walking through the jungle, if you come across a snake on the ground, _____ calm and leave it well alone. It will not attack you.
3. When you meet my father, remember to say "please" and "thank you". He's a bit _____ and old-fashioned, but he's very likeable.
4. I have to go to the police station and give them a _____ about the accident which I witnessed in the high road yesterday.
5. Your brother was seriously injured in the accident, but at the moment his condition is _____ and he's not in any immediate danger.
6. We are getting reports of an accident on the main road out of the city. All the traffic is _____, with queues for about three kilometres.
7. We can see how the president's _____ as an effective politician has grown since he dealt with the terrorist threat so successfully.
8. A lot of people claim that wealth doesn't increase your _____ in society, but I think it does. Money can get you everywhere.
9. The government can propose a law, but it's only when parliament votes on it that it can actually become law and go on the _____ book.
10. According to the latest road _____, the accident rate in this city has fallen significantly since the introduction of speed cameras.
11. We went to see a new house this morning. It's in a really nice part of town with a nice garden, but it's in a poor _____ of repair and needs lots of work.
12. I'm really nervous. This is my first time on _____ in front of such a big audience. I hope I remember all my lines in the play.

102

72. stare 2

Put the most suitable word in each space. Think about the part of speech required in each space. Make sure you use the correct form.

assist, coexist, consist, consistency, desist, exist, existence, insist, persist,
persistent, resist, subsist

1. Millions of people around the world are so poor that they find it really hard to
   _____ on less than a dollar a day.

2. If you need anyone to _____ you with your book search, just come
   and ask for help at the library enquiry desk.

3. So many people around the world have different beliefs and ways of life that we
   have to be very tolerant if we are to _____ in peace.

4. When the police came to Morris's house, he tried to _____ arrest,
   so they had to get him into the police van forcibly, and that's when he was hurt.

5. My English class _____ mainly of students from European
   countries, but there are some from South America and Japan as well.

6. Excuse me, if you _____ in shouting and interrupting the speech,
   I'll have to ask you to leave the hall and not come back.

7. The letter from the lawyer says if you do not _____ from making
   false accusations against his client, he will sue you for defamation of character.

8. I'm sorry, but I'm not at all happy with the service in this store. I
   _____ on speaking to the manager immediately.

9. If the _____ of the cake mix is too thick and stodgy, then add milk
   little by little until it becomes thinner and smoother.

10. Scientists at the space research institute are looking for radio signals from
    space to find evidence for the _____ of intelligent life out there.

11. When you start training seriously in sport it's really hard on your body, but you
    have to be _____ and not give up if you want to succeed.

12. Children today are really surprised when I tell them that computers and game
    systems didn't _____ when I was a boy.

73. stare 3

Put the most suitable word in each space. Think about the part of speech required in each space. Make sure you use the correct form.

constituency, constitute, constitution, destitute, institute, institution, institutional, prostitution, restitution, substitute, superstition, superstitious

1. Can you believe that? Martin's so _____ that he refuses to cross the road, because he saw a black cat going from left to right.
2. This course _____ a major part of your final degree, so you have to make sure you do all the coursework and prepare properly for the exam.
3. When I saw the way that the poor people in the mountains were living, I was horrified. They're so _____ they don't even have tents for shelter.
4. After the revolution, the new government started reforming all the essential _____ of government, like the health and education systems.
5. My grandfather is eighty-five now, but he still walks in the hills up to ten miles a day. He's got an amazing _____ for his age. He never gets ill.
6. I'm afraid that the original speaker is ill and cannot attend the conference, but we have a very able _____ in Professor Simms.
7. After Joanna left school, she got into bad company. She started taking drugs, and soon turned to _____ to finance her drug habit.
8. After he sold his software business, Bob Walls used some of his money to set up a new training _____ to help poor children prepare for working life.
9. I never look at my horoscope. I don't believe in astrology at all. It's just a big collection of _____ and has no connection with reality.
10. The police were accused of _____ racism, when they failed as an organisation to investigate properly the murder of a young black man.
11. In the UK, every Member of Parliament is elected to represent one of over 640 _____, which are electoral divisions of cities and country areas.
12. The Greek government has asked the British Museum for the _____ of the artefacts which were removed by British archaeologists 200 years ago.

74. stare 4

Put the most suitable word in each space. Think about the part of speech required in each space. Make sure you use the correct form.

arrest, contrast, destination, destine, destiny, establish, estate, obstacle, obstinate, predestined, rest, restate

1. Remember that it's very difficult for new lawyers to rise to the top of the legal profession. There'll be many _____ for you to overcome.

2. If we _____ last year's results with this year's, we can see how much the students' performance has improved.

3. When Liam and Sandra met for the first time, they fell in love immediately. It seemed to them that they were _____ to be together.

4. When my grandmother died, she left a large _____ of over £10 million in investments and property, which was shared out among her six grandchildren.

5. Did you understand everything I explained about the course, or do you want me to _____ it all to you?

6. Our final _____ is Tokyo, but we have to change planes in Paris and we're stopping over for a few days in Dubai.

7. Why do you have to be so _____? I'm not asking you to do anything difficult, so I don't understand why you're refusing to help.

8. Some people believe that everything in your life is _____ and there's nothing that you can do to change it, so there's no point in trying.

9. I want to use the money from selling my company to _____ a new training centre, so that talented children can get specialist training in sport.

10. I can give you half of the money today and the _____ of the money next week. Is that OK?

11. From a young age, Bob Clapton believed that it was his _____ to become the president, so when he was elected, he felt it was fulfilled.

12. This is the police! Put down your weapons and come out of the building slowly with your hands up. You're under _____!

75. stare 5

Put the most suitable word in each space. Think about the part of speech required in each space. Make sure you use the correct form.

circumstance, circumstantial, constant, distance, extant, instance, instant, instantaneous, stance, staunch, substance, substantial

1. Many of the plays of the great Greek dramatist, Sophocles, were lost, but his _____ plays are still widely performed today.

2. As a result of the rising price of oil, there has been a _____ increase in the price of petrol this year, at least 10%.

3. I used to be a _____ supporter of this government and I agreed with everything they said, but the more they change, the less I support them.

4. The police wanted to arrest Morris as a murder suspect, but the evidence against him was purely _____, with nothing concrete linking him to the case.

5. I've really had enough of that _____ loud music from the flat next door. I have to put up with it day and night. I wish they'd stop.

6. I really hate _____ coffee. It's quick to make, but it tastes awful. You need time to make a really good cup of coffee from freshly ground beans.

7. This speed of this car is really amazing. The moment you start the car and put your foot down, the acceleration is _____, like a jet plane.

8. Although the _____ from here to the nearest town in a straight line is only ten kilometres, the river winds so much that it's almost 20km by boat.

9. Although we know roughly when and where the little girl disappeared, we don't know the exact _____ of her disappearance.

10. Although many people believe that sharks are dangerous, there have actually been relatively few _____ of sharks attacking people.

11. I would like to remind you all that the college takes a firm _____ against any form of academic misconduct, such as plagiarism and copying.

12. Scientists claim to have invented a new _____ in the laboratory, which is stronger than steel and more flexible than rubber.

76. tempus

Put the most suitable word in each space. Think about the part of speech required in each space. Make sure you use the correct form.

contemporary, extemporise, temper (2), temperance, temperament, temperate, temperature, tempo, temporal, temporary, tense

1. Have you seen that new science fiction film, Timeshift? These astronauts are thrown into the past through a _____ shift and try to get back to the present.

2. My speech to the college last night was almost a disaster. I lost all my notes and had to _____, but I luckily I managed to pull it off it in the end.

3. I know you really want to get this job, but you have to _____ your enthusiasm in the interview so that you can give a good impression.

4. I've read classical English literature from Shakespeare onwards, but I much prefer _____ writing, especially the novels from the last ten years.

5. I don't think you have the right _____ to be a teacher. You have to be far more committed, patient and understanding than you are at the moment.

6. My uncle used to drink a lot of alcohol and it almost ruined him. Then he stopped and now he's a great advocate of _____. He hasn't drunk in years.

7. You can move in for a while, but it's only a _____ arrangement. You have to find your own place by next month as my flatmate's coming back.

8. In many languages, including English, some _____ can be used to refer to more than one time, like the present and the future.

9. My ex-husband's actually a nice man, but he's got a terrible _____. He always shouted at me when he got angry, and that's mainly why I left him.

10. I don't really like this version of Beethoven's fifth symphony. I find that the conductor plays it at too high a _____. It should be slower.

11. Tomorrow will be fine and dry, with plenty of sun and a light breeze. The _____ will range from 16C to 25C.

12. Britain lies in a _____ zone, where the winters are never very cold and the summers are never very hot.

77. tendere 1

Put the most suitable word in each space. Think about the part of speech required in each space. Make sure you use the correct form.

attend, attention, attentive, tend, tendency, tendentious, tender, tense (2), tensile, tension, tent

1. Remember that if you don't _____ every class on the course you won't be entered for the exam at the end.

2. We've decided to go on a camping holiday next summer, so we need a new family _____. Do you know where we can buy a good one?

3. The steel used to make these chains has a very high _____ strength. They can carry tonnes without breaking.

4. The atmosphere in the stadium is so _____ that you can cut it with a knife. The next penalty in this shoot-out will win the World Cup.

5. I can't meet you for certain on Wednesday afternoon, because at that time we _____ to have college meetings. Is Thursday OK?

6. My son's school report says he's doing well generally, but he has to be more _____ in class, as he often misses what the teacher says.

7. The financial manager took full responsibility for the losses and decided to _____ his resignation at the emergency meeting.

8. I like Sandra, but sometime she really annoys me, especially when she talks loud and waves her hands, like she's seeking _____.

9. The new talks are being held to reduce the _____ on the border between the two countries, which are threatening to start another war.

10. The latest government statistics on family life show that there is a greater _____ these days for couples to live together without marrying.

11. George loves making deliberately _____ statements when he's discussing things, because it really makes other people react so much.

12. You have to learn to relax if you're going to perform to your best. You can't run your fastest if you _____ up before every race.

78. tendere 2

Put the most suitable word in each space. Think about the part of speech required in each space. Make sure you use the correct form.

contend, contention, contentious, détente, distended, entente, extend, extension, extensive, portend, portent, tend

1. At the moment the economic signals do not _____ well for the future. There are likely to be more problems ahead for the economy.

2. In the 1970s, the USA and the USSR pursued a policy of _____, aimed at making the different political systems exist more easily with each other.

3. As a result of the problems that the students have had with accessing the internet for their research, we have _____ the deadline for their submissions.

4. You claim that you were nowhere near the house at the time of the crime, but it is my _____ that you were there and took part in it. Am I not right?

5. You can clearly see the signs of malnutrition in the children at the refugee camp. Their _____ stomachs show how little they have eaten recently.

6. After the accident, the police closed off the road and paramedics arrived in their ambulances to _____ to the people injured in the crash.

7. In ancient times, superstitious people like the Romans regarded the actions of animals and birds as _____ to guide their future actions.

8. To avoid future conflicts, the three neighbouring countries entered into a special _____, by which they would discuss mutual problems together.

9. My grandfather left all his money to me in his will, but my brother has decided to _____ it and claim half of the money.

10. We've got permission to build a new _____ to our house. We're going to use it as a giant play room for the children.

11. The question of a fee increase is a very _____ issue. Most of our members agree with our proposals, but there are some who disagree strongly.

12. Tomorrow will start very dull, with rain in the south, but during the day, the clouds will break and there will be _____ sunshine.

79. tendere 3

Put the most suitable word in each space. Think about the part of speech required in each space. Make sure you use the correct form.

intend, intense, intensify, intensity, intensive, intent, intention, ostensibly, ostentatious, pretence, pretend, pretentious

1. All those film stars at the Oscar presentations are so _____. They all want to be the centre of attention with their clothes and jewellery.
2. I'm sure you've heard rumours that I'm going to leave my position as manager of this football club, but actually I have no _____ of leaving.
3. I'm being sent to our new office in Moscow, so I have to go on a two-week _____ course in Russian to learn the basics before I go to Russia.
4. While their children were growing up, Tom and June kept up the _____ of a happy marriage, but after the children left home, they got divorced.
5. It's best to stay in the shade and not on the beach between 10.00 and 3.00, because the _____ of the sunshine is at its greatest.
6. My daughter went out at 6.00, _____ to visit her friend, but someone saw her at the station with a strange man, and now she's disappeared.
7. I know you think you're under pressure now, but as you get closer to the exams, it's going to _____, so you should start revising for them soon.
8. When Harry was arrested, the police found a knife on him, so he was charged with possession of a dangerous weapon with _____ to harm.
9. I really hate it when people drop French words into their conversations and try to come across as really cultured. In actual fact, it's really so _____.
10. I've been working in this job for so long now, I need a new challenge. So I _____ to emigrate to Australia next year to start a new life.
11. If you see a bear and it starts chasing you, lie down and _____ to be dead, and it will lose interest and go away.
12. John has had an _____ fear of spiders ever since he woke up one night with one on his face. He runs a mile if he sees one.

80. tenere 1

Put the most suitable word in each space. Think about the part of speech required in each space. Make sure you use the correct form.

countenance, maintain, maintenance, pertain, pertinent, tenable, tenacious, tenant, tenement, tenet, tenor, tenure

1. One of the main _____ of our educational system is that every child should have the same opportunities to learn and succeed in life.
2. In the 1960s, the local council built a lot of _____ blocks of flats for poorer people to live in, but people generally didn't like living in them.
3. Ever since he was a child, Joe Watkins wanted to be a great singer, and now he's developed into the greatest operatic _____ of modern times.
4. He's such a _____ fighter. Whenever you think he's going to lose a boxing match, he comes back and fights on. He never knows when he's beaten.
5. I know the company is going through difficult times at the moment, but I'm going to stick with it. I wouldn't _____ selling it now or at any time in the future.
6. The company has received a serious complaint against you. It _____ to your treatment of a customer on the phone last Friday.
7. After the terrible company performance over the last few months, we felt that the manager's position was no longer _____, so he has resigned.
8. We can't talk about finance at this meeting as it's not _____ to the subject under discussion, which is course timetabling for next year.
9. This is just to let you know that the college computer system will be down in the morning for the technicians to perform routine _____.
10. The landlord has written to all the _____ in the apartment block to tell them that there is going to be a rent increase of 10%.
11. At our college, we try hard to _____ the high standards of education that we have achieved over the past few years.
12. At the end of his ten year _____ of the post, the Prime Minister announced that he would step down at the next election.

81. tenere 2

Put the most suitable word in each space. Think about the part of speech required in each space. Make sure you use the correct form.

abstain, abstention, continue, detain, detention, discontinue, entertain, lieutenant, retain, retention, retentive, retinue

1. Jimmy can't come out on Saturday morning. He's got two hours' _____ at school because he came late three times this week.

2. Everywhere she goes, Marilena has a massive _____ of about 50 helpers and assistants following her. It's like she's a queen and not a pop star.

3. The only real way to beat alcoholism is _____. As long as you can stay off the drink, you'll do well, but you'll need a lot of help.

4. I'm sorry, but we don't stock that make of washing machine at this store any more. It was _____ last year after sales fell too low.

5. After the captain was killed in an ambush by enemy soldiers, the _____ took command and led the soldiers back to safety.

6. The college is working hard to increase enrolment and student _____. Last year we kept more students on our courses than in any year before.

7. It's almost 1.00, so let's take a break now and then we can _____ the discussions after lunch.

8. You've got a great voice, you know. Have you ever _____ the idea of auditioning for a part in that new musical? I think you'd have a good chance.

9. Immigration officials have _____ two men who arrived at Heathrow Airport this morning without passports and with suitcases full of money.

10. Your operation is scheduled for Friday morning. Could you please make sure that you _____ from all food and drink from 8.00 on Thursday?

11. As I get older my memory is not as _____ as it used to be, so I find I have to write things down a lot more to remember them.

12. I know Jones is 32 now, and he's not as fast a player as he used to be, but he still _____ a high level of skill, fitness and intelligence.

82. tenere 3

Put the most suitable word in each space. Think about the part of speech required in each space. Make sure you use the correct form.

contain, containment, content (2), contentment, continent, continental, discontent, obtain, subcontinent, sustain, sustenance

1. Children need enough _____ to get them through the day. This means three good meals a day, with small snacks in between.

2. The fact that the president's popularity is now only 25% shows the high level of _____ that the people feel with his policies.

3. One of the most fascinating aspects of Istanbul is its position as the bridge between the _____ of Europe and Asia.

4. When you plan your course project, you need to make sure that you do research and find enough good _____ to put in it before you start writing.

5. The more I listened to the manager telling me how to do my job, the harder it was for me to _____ my anger, until I finally lost my temper.

6. I could see Terry's huge _____ with life, as he sat by the side of his swimming pool, with a drink and a cigar, and a big smile on his face.

7. This country has a typical _____ climate, with long, hot summers and long, cold winters.

8. You can ask anyone you like. Most people aren't _____ with their lives as they are, and are working hard to earn money and improve their living standards.

9. Some of the most popular dishes in modern Britain have their origins in the Indian _____ and were brought in by immigrants.

10. To _____ a new driving licence, you need to fill in a form and send it to the office with your old one, along with two photographs.

11. Horton is playing such a high-powered game of tennis today that I don't think he can _____ it for the whole match. He's sure to get tired soon.

12. The government is worried about the growing number of strikes and is working on a policy of _____ to try to stop them spreading.

83. terminus

Put the most suitable word in each space. Think about the part of speech required in each space. Make sure you use the correct form.

determine, determined, indeterminate, interminable, predetermined, term (2), terminal (2), terminate, terminology, terminus

1. One of the most important things about studying a subject at university is to learn the related _____, so that you can understand it well enough.

2. Maria is arriving today on the bus from Madrid. I'm going to meet her at the bus _____, because she's never been to this city before.

3. Police investigating the failed bombing attempts in the city last week said the bombers had planned to set them off together at a _____ time.

4. Last summer we got caught up in the airport strikes. The worst thing is the _____ wait without knowing when you'll get away.

5. After Zak was diagnosed with _____ cancer, he decided to sell up everything and travel the world for one last time before he died.

6. We've been looking at the current project in great detail and I'm afraid we'll have to _____ it next month, as the results are below our expectations.

7. Archaeologists claim that at an _____ time in the past eighty thousand years, humans first moved out of Africa into Asia.

8. Joyce has decided to get a DNA test for the baby to _____ once and for all whether the father is Lawrence or Graham.

9. I've been reading this biology book for my course, but there's a _____ here that I don't understand. It's not in the dictionary. Do you know what it is?

10. In the USA, the president is elected for a fixed _____ of four years, but in the UK, the Prime Minister is elected for a maximum of five years.

11. My plane arrives in London Airport at 3.15 at _____ 4. Please make sure you can meet me there, as I've got lots of luggage.

12. You could see from a very early age that David was absolutely _____ to become a footballer, and nothing would stop him.

84. terra

Put the most suitable word in each space. Think about the part of speech required in each space. Make sure you use the correct form.

disinter, extraterrestrial, inter, Mediterranean, subterranean, terrace, terracotta, terrain, terrestrial, territorial, territory

1. The planned expedition will take two weeks, covering some of the most difficult desert and mountain _____ in the country.

2. Archaeologists in Peru have found the body of a 2500-year-old woman, who was _____ with huge amounts of gold and jewellery.

3. This year we're thinking of going on holiday to a _____ country, possibly Spain, Italy or Greece.

4. Scientists examining strange rocks from the site of yesterday's explosion confirmed that they are of _____ origin and not from space.

5. The cave leads deep into the ground, where there are _____ passages running through the base of the mountain.

6. Although Britain no longer has an empire, it still controls a small number of overseas_____ dotted around the world, like St Helena.

7. We went around a local market near our hotel, where we found some beautiful brown _____ vases and bowls made by the local people.

8. Most of the houses in the street were built in a long _____ two hundred years ago to house workers in the local coal mine.

9. After the discovery of new evidence, police have decided to _____ and re-examine the body of Larry Moore, who was murdered in the city last year.

10. Two countries have made claims to the oil-rich Midsea Islands and are threatening to go to war if the _____ dispute is not settled soon.

11. In John Laker's latest film, a young boy walking in the woods late in the evening comes across a large spacecraft with a strange _____ being in it.

85. trahere 1

Put the most suitable word in each space. Think about the part of speech required in each space. Make sure you use the correct form.

trace, tract, tractable, traction, tractor, trail, train, trait, treat, treatise, treatment, treaty

1. In the past, farmers had to use horses or oxen to plough fields, but these days most farmers use a _____, which is much more efficient.

2. Police are trying to _____ the parents of a young boy who was found wandering along a country road in the middle of last night.

3. It's a pity John's decided to leave the company. He was a great manager. He always tried to _____ all the staff carefully and fairly.

4. Can you wait a moment? I'm concentrating on something and I don't want to break my _____ of thought, or I'll forget it.

5. The hunter shot at the reindeer, but it ran away. However, he managed to find it by following the _____ of blood in the snow.

6. After the war, representatives from all the countries sat down and negotiated a new peace _____, which they hoped would avoid conflict in the future.

7. You'll find that Howard is not a very _____ person in his business dealings. You have to try hard to persuade him that your ideas are workable.

8. The problem with hospitals in this country is that they are too crowded and under pressure. You have to pay for the best medical _____.

9. In motor racing you have to know what the weather will be like before the race, because the wrong tyres will have no _____ on the ground in rain.

10. When I first went to Australia, I was amazed as the plane flew for hundreds of miles across vast _____ of desert and uninhabited land.

11. While he was a lecturer at this university, Professor Higgins wrote his famous _____ on the changes in social life in the modern world.

12. One of the most likeable character _____ of this dog is its ability to get on well with children. It's the perfect family pet.

86. trahere 2

Put the most suitable word in each space. Think about the part of speech required in each space. Make sure you use the correct form.

abstract (2), abstraction, contract (2), contraction, contractual, portrait, portray, retrace, retreat, subcontract

1. The problem with the press these days is they try to _____ politicians as lazy, greedy and dishonest, while most of them are not like that.

2. While my father was working in equatorial Africa, he _____ malaria and had to be sent home to recover, though it still affects him from time to time.

3. If you want to know what a book is about before you buy it, you can read an _____ on the publisher's website. It will give you a basic idea of it.

4. I don't like this job any more, but I have a _____ obligation to give three months' notice before I can leave, so I'll just have to stick it out till then.

5. We're planning to go on an expedition to Antarctica, to try to _____ the route that Captain Scott took in his attempt to reach the South Pole.

6. When my wife's _____ started, we knew the baby was coming, so I drove her to the hospital as fast as I could. The baby arrived half an hour later.

7. When it became clear that the enemy were winning, the commander ordered his troops to _____ back to the camp and regroup.

8. The problem with many employment _____ these days is that neither the employers nor the employees respect them or work to them.

9. The most famous painting in the world is Leonardo Da Vinci's famous _____ of the Mona Lisa, which hangs in the Louvre in Paris.

10. When we started the job to build 10,000 computers, we realised that we couldn't complete them all on time, so we _____ some to another company.

11. It's not known exactly when children are first capable of _____ thought, but they are certainly capable of it by the time they are five.

12. In the early part of the 20th century, artists increasingly painted their own _____ of reality rather than reality itself.

87. trahere 3

Put the most suitable word in each space. Think about the part of speech required in each space. Make sure you use the correct form.

attract, attraction, attractive, detract, detractor, distract, distraction, distraught, extract, protracted, retract, subtract

1. I'm going to the library to study. I can't concentrate enough at home. There are too many _____, like the TV and my flatmates talking all the time.
2. Simpson has had a lot of criticism for his poor form on the tennis court recently, but this emphatic championship win will silence his _____.
3. As soon as the fruit is picked, it is put in a special machine to _____ the pulp, which is then dried, packed and sent to the shops.
4. We need to find new ways to _____ customers onto the trains when it's quieter during the day, so we plan to issue a new daytime travel card.
5. To find out how much tax you need to pay, first you _____ your tax-free £500 from your monthly salary, and then divide the rest by 25%.
6. At first Josh didn't want to sell me his shares in the company, but the offer I made him was so _____ that he couldn't refuse it.
7. I was very angry when that critic made those comments and accusations about me, but now that he has _____ them, I'm happy to forget about it.
8. Can you children sit quietly in the back of the car? It's difficult to find my way around this town, and I don't want you to _____ me from my driving.
9. We're going to have a summer fete in the school, with competitions, sports, animal performances and lots of other _____.
10. The turbulence on the flight was so bad that by the time our plane landed, the woman sitting next to me was absolutely _____ with fear.
11. After a _____ delay of over an hour, as the result of an accident right outside the football stadium, the match finally started at 9.00.
12. I don't want to _____ from your undoubted success, but I think you made some basic mistakes and can perform far better in the future.

118

88. vivere

Put the most suitable word in each space. Think about the part of speech required in each space. Make sure you use the correct form.

convivial, revitalise, revival, revive, survival, survive, viable, vital, vitality, vitamin, vivacious, vivid

1. The problem with my business was that it had lost so much money, it wasn't _____ any more, so the only option was to close it down.

2. I was feeling really run down, so I had a quiet, relaxing week off work at a hotel in the country. It's really _____ me and I'm ready for anything.

3. The thing I really like about Jenny is she's such a _____ and sociable person. She's wonderful to be with. You really have to meet her.

4. When they found Joanna in her bedroom, she was unconscious, with an empty bottle of sleeping pills next to her, but they managed to _____ her.

5. Though your grandfather and I married over 50 years ago, the memory of the wedding is still so _____ in my mind that it's as if it were yesterday.

6. You shouldn't cook fresh vegetables for too long, because if you do, you lose a lot of the _____ and minerals that they contain.

7. I used to sit at home eating fast food and watching TV, but since I changed my diet and joined a health club, my _____ has really increased.

8. Tigers everywhere are in danger of extinction, and their _____ depends on us. We need to set up forest reserves to protect them.

9. Sport and physical exercise are _____ to the health and wellbeing of children as they grow up. Without them, their bodies can't develop properly.

10. Football was in decline in Britain in the 1980s, but with big TV money, international players and new stadiums, there was a huge _____ in the 1990s.

11. Although this was the annual general meeting of the society, there was a really _____ atmosphere, with lots of food, drink, music and dancing.

12. When the Titanic sank on its first voyage to America, only a few hundred people _____. Most passengers drowned or died from cold.

89. vocare, vox 1

Put the most suitable word in each space. Think about the part of speech required in each space. Make sure you use the correct form.

vocabulary, vocal, vocalise, vocalist, vocation, vocational, vociferous, voice (2), vouch, voucher, vowel

1. After my father had his stroke, it affected his speech in such a way that he found it difficult to _____ exactly what he was thinking.

2. Although English has five _____ in the written alphabet, there are actually twenty of them in the pronunciation system.

3. The college is going to start ten new _____ courses next term, ranging from business studies to hairdressing and car mechanics.

4. Peter has been a very _____ campaigner for animal rights, and has spoken out against animal research on many occasions.

5. As my train was delayed for over an hour, the train company compensated me by giving me a special _____ to take a free journey next month.

6. I replied to an advert for a _____ in a new band, and when I auditioned, they liked my singing so much that they invited me to join.

7. At the public meeting, most people calmly discussed the problem, but one man was so _____ that he shouted all the time and was asked to leave.

8. From a very early age my brother felt his _____ in life was to become a fire-fighter, and now he's managed to get onto a training course.

9. I know Jim didn't stay on the course and finish it last time he took it, but he says he's more committed to it now, and I can _____ for him. Trust me.

10. When you are learning a language, you should try to learn at least twenty new words a week so that you can quickly increase your _____.

11. This political party was formed a century ago to give a _____ to all the poor and the workers in the country, and we must never forget that.

12. The Prince of Wales today _____ his displeasure with the type of poor education that he felt children were being given in schools.

90. vocare, vox 2

Put the most suitable word in each space. Think about the part of speech required in each space. Make sure you use the correct form.

advocate (2), convocation, equivocal, evocative, evoke, invocation, invoke, provocation, provocative, provoke, revoke

1. The government was very worried about violence at the demonstration outside the Houses of Parliament, so they _____ an ancient law to ban it.

2. When I asked the minister about the reports of his resignation, his response was _____, neither confirming nor denying them.

3. All the students and lecturers will attend the _____ at the end of the college year to give out the students' degrees and diplomas.

4. During her whole life, Emma Porthouse was a strong _____ of equal rights for women in all areas of society and culture.

5. In the political debate, one of the candidates made some very _____ remarks about one of the others, leading to a heated argument between them.

6. As I listened to the Beatles' songs again, they _____ memories of my childhood growing up in the 1960s in Liverpool. They were such happy times.

7. The judge decided to free the prisoner on licence, as long as he stayed out of trouble, otherwise his licence would be _____.

8. You shouldn't _____ the dog when he's eating. He might react badly, and you don't want him to bite you.

9. I find these paintings of old England very _____. They speak to me of times when life was simpler, slower and more in tune with nature.

10. The judge didn't jail the defendant, because she accepted his argument that he attacked the victim as a result of extreme _____.

11. At the start of the ceremony, the priests made a powerful _____ to their gods to grant them fair weather and a good harvest.

12. As your leader, I would never _____ the use of force to achieve our goals. We need to use only peaceful protest and resistance.

91. civis, colere

Put the most suitable word in each space. Think about the part of speech required in each space. Make sure you use the correct form.

citizen, city, civic, civil, civilian, civilisation, civility; colonial, colony, cult, cultivate, culture

1. In the 17th and 18th century Britain established _____ in many parts of the world, including America, the Caribbean and Australia.

2. Explorers in the Mexican jungle have discovered a great city, which they believe belonged to the lost Mayan _____ of eight hundred years ago.

3. Over the last fifty years, British _____ has changed a great deal, especially in the areas of music, food, fashion and art.

4. If you live here for five years and you are of good character, you can make an application to become a _____ of this country.

5. The problem these days is that people are less and less considerate and polite. People need to show more _____ to each other.

6. Nowadays, life in the _____ is getting more and more difficult and dangerous. I'm going to live in the countryside, where it's safer and quieter.

7. Most of the Hispanic countries of South America fought hard for independence from their _____ power, which was Spain.

8. Following the _____ war in England, in which Parliamentary forces defeated the Royalists, the king was executed and the monarchy was abolished.

9. Although most of Egypt is desert, the River Nile floods every year and allows the people to _____ a variety of crops on the rich land along the river.

10. One of the biggest problems for many soldiers to deal with is leaving the army and becoming a _____ again. Many soldiers fail to adjust.

11. Police have arrested Karl Tobin, the leader of a religious _____ known as the Millennium Brigade, which has been planning a bombing campaign.

12. The town council is planning to build a new _____ centre, which will house the town hall, council offices, the library and the sports centre.

92. damnum, durus

Put the most suitable word in each space. Think about the part of speech required in each space. Make sure you use the correct form.

condemn, damage, damages, damn, indemnity; dour, durable, duration, duress, during, endure, obdurate

1. I can't understand Ken's attitude sometimes. It's so hard to get him to agree to anything. He's one of the most _____ people I've ever met.
2. Graham Black has the public image of a _____, humourless and hard-working politician, but in private he's actually really enjoyable company.
3. After Hurricane Eliza passed through Florida last week, the government estimates that it caused over $1 billion worth of _____ to property.
4. Oh, _____ it! I forgot to lock the door when we left the house. How could I forget? We'll have to go all the way back home and do it.
5. These boots are extremely _____. You can wear them every day and walk on all kinds of terrain, and they'll last for ages. The army use them.
6. This insurance provides you with full _____ for any injury or loss on your holiday, with a payment of up to £500,000.
7. Though Ian drove the car in the bank robbery, he said he only did it under immense _____, because the others threatened to kill him if he refused.
8. It's amazing to think that this temple was built by the Egyptians over three thousand years ago and it's _____ till now in such good condition.
9. This is your guide, Thomas. He's going to accompany you and help you find your way around for the _____ of your stay in this country.
10. The Prime Minister has _____ the comments of the leader of the opposition, who accused him of lying about the true state of the economy.
11. These desert foxes sleep _____ the day, but as soon as night falls, they come out and hunt for rats and mice.
12. At the end of the court case about my ruined trip, the judge ruled in my favour and told the travel agent to pay me £500 in _____ for my losses.

93. fallere, fendere

Put the most suitable word in each space. Think about the part of speech required in each space. Make sure you use the correct form.

default, fail, fallacy, fallible, false, falsify, fault; defence, defend, fend, offence, offend

1. Look! There's no point arguing about whose _____ it is that we forgot the passports. It's done, and we just have to go home and get them.

2. It's important that you learn about the customs and culture of any countries you travel to, to avoid causing _____ to anyone.

3. Did you hear about our manager? He was sacked after our accountant found out that he had _____ his expenses on his last trip.

4. If you let me manage this project, I promise I won't _____ you. You know you can rely on me to make sure the project is completely successful.

5. The problem with this football team isn't with the attack. That's playing really well. We really need to _____ far better to stop conceding goals.

6. Don't believe Jack when he says that he'll do something for you. He's always giving _____ promises and never actually does what he says he'll do.

7. Someone tried to take my mobile phone just after I got off the bus, but I managed to _____ him off and he ran away without it.

8. A lot of people believe that you get fat if you eat late at night, but actually it's a complete _____. It makes no difference when you eat, but how much.

9. Don't forget that, even if someone is highly qualified and experienced, they can still make mistakes. Even the best experts are _____ sometimes.

10. The problem with the criminal justice system is that 80% of ex-prisoners go on to _____ again at least once after they come out.

11. I know Peter has made a lot of mistakes, but in his _____, he is new to the job and he's trying hard to learn and put things right.

12. Can you lend me £1000? I have to make my next mortgage payment by next week, and I might lose the house if I _____ on it again.

94. labor, liber

Put the most suitable word in each space. Think about the part of speech required in each space. Make sure you use the correct form.

collaborate, elaborate, laboratory, laborious, labour; deliver, illiberal, liberal, liberate, libertarian, libertine, liberty

1. Dr Jekyll is not available at the moment. He's conducting an important experiment in the _____ and can't be disturbed until tomorrow morning.

2. If a company promises a client that they'll complete a job by a certain time, then they have to _____. There should be no excuses if they don't.

3. We had to sort through all the old stuff in the storeroom and decide whether to keep it or throw it out. It was really _____ and boring work.

4. Casanova was the most famous _____ in history. His adventures with women and drink are legendary. He really had very few morals.

5. Have you heard the news? Our university has made an agreement with London University to _____ on the new computer project. It's so exciting!

6. I'm not going to vote for Jim Hedge for President. I think his views on issues like equality and immigration are really _____ and reactionary.

7. The government is trying to find ways of ensuring that the country is secure against terrorist attack, without affecting people's individual _____.

8. The last president had very _____ policies. One of the most important things he did was to provide free health care to poor people.

9. The problem with the course application system is that new students find it far too _____. We need to find ways to simplify and streamline it.

10. His attitude is very _____. He says people must not be restricted from doing what they want and saying what they think, no matter what.

11. The factory relies a lot on casual _____, because the work is not regular enough for it to employ people on a permanent basis.

12. The D-Day invasion of Normandy in June 1944 was the first act in the allied campaign to _____ Europe from Nazi occupation.

95. mirus, mutare

Put the most suitable word in each space. Think about the part of speech required in each space. Make sure you use the correct form.

admire, marvellous, miracle, miraculous, mirage, mirror; commute, commuter, mutant, mutate, mutual, permutation

1. Neil Hutton was originally sentenced to death for murder, but the sentence was eventually _____ by the judge to life imprisonment.

2. I found that documentary on homeless people really fascinating. It managed to hold up a _____ for society to look at itself, and it wasn't nice.

3. Scientists are worried that the influenza virus has _____ into a new strain, so that the vaccine used last year might not be effective against it.

4. I visited the new neighbour yesterday. She's really decorated her house nicely and the furniture's lovely. I really _____ her taste.

5. Just a week ago, the doctors thought that my mother wouldn't survive the operation, but she's made an almost _____ recovery. She'll be home next week.

6. This election is so difficult to predict. With all the small parties, there are so many _____ that no one knows how it will turn out and who will govern.

7. People lost in the desert often think they can see an oasis, but it isn't really there. It's just a _____, which results from heat and exhaustion.

8. Scientists have made a breakthrough in their search for a cure for lung cancer. They have found a _____ gene which might be a cause of it.

9. We had a really _____ time on our holiday. The hotel was great, the weather was lovely and the food was really delicious.

10. I met a really interesting guy at the party last night. We found out that we had a _____ interest in horror films, so we're going to one tomorrow.

11. Three engines on the plane cut out, so the pilot had to land it on only one engine, but we got down safely. It was a _____ we didn't crash.

12. There's going to be another train strike tomorrow, so it's going to be very difficult for _____ to get to work on time in the morning.

96. pretium, proprius

Put the most suitable word in each space. Think about the part of speech required in each space. Make sure you use the correct form.

appraise, appreciate, appreciative, praise, precious, price, prize; appropriate, expropriate, proper, property, proprietor

1. Could you just fill in your name, address and email here? We will enter you into the competition and you can win a _____ of £1000.
2. It is important for parents to _____ their children when they learn to do new things and when they do things the right way. It encourages them to learn more.
3. I found a mobile phone in the street yesterday. I found out who it belonged to and took it round to the owner, who was very _____.
4. The local council gave the squatters a month's notice to leave. When they didn't, it simply _____ the illegally occupied buildings and threw them out.
5. I was very grateful to be able to come home and spend those last few _____ days with my grandfather before he died.
6. If you go for a job interview, you need to wear _____ clothes, like a suit, a shirt, a tie and black shoes.
7. Have you heard the latest news? Our company has been sold, and the new _____ is calling a meeting tomorrow to tell us his plans.
8. We need to _____ the financial situation in the company in detail before we decide what steps we need to take to improve it.
9. I'm going to France to buy a house. The _____ there is much cheaper than in Britain, and you get a lot more for your money.
10. That's not the _____ way to ask somebody for something. You should always say "please" and "thank you", or you'll sound rude.
11. Your house is in good condition, but it needs cleaning and redecorating. Then you should get a good _____ when you sell it.
12. I don't think you really _____ how much I've done to help you. If you did, you wouldn't complain all the time about everything I do.

97. sanus, satis

Put the most suitable word in each space. Think about the part of speech required in each space. Make sure you use the correct form.

sanatorium, sane, sanitation, sanitise, sanity, unsanitary; asset, dissatisfied, satiate, satisfaction, satisfy, saturate

1. The company's annual report has been completely _____. There's nothing in it about the bad management and poor staff performance.

2. My clothes are completely _____. I forgot to take my umbrella and got caught in the rain on the way here. Where can I dry off?

3. We have a serious problem with _____. The toilets aren't working properly and they're really dirty. Something needs to be done about it.

4. The lion feasted on the dead zebra while the vultures looked on hungrily. When its hunger was _____, it left the zebra to the other animals.

5. Our new secretary is a real _____ to the company. She does things so efficiently and correctly that everything works really smoothly.

6. I have to leave this job. Working in this place is driving me crazy. I just can't do it any more. It's beginning to affect my _____.

7. Waiter! This steak has not been cooked to my _____. I asked for it to be well done, but it's still rare. Get me another one.

8. I've been working so hard I need a complete break for a few weeks, so my company is sending me to a _____ by the sea to rest and recharge my batteries.

9. When we receive the applications for the job, we have to look through them carefully to ensure that they _____ the requirements.

10. You can't really be serious about this plan you have to swim solo to America. Any _____ person can see it's a crazy idea. You'll never make it.

11. My boss is so difficult to please. It doesn't matter how well I do my work, he's always _____ with some aspect of it and complains.

12. I went to visit my sick father in hospital yesterday and I was horrified to see just how _____ the conditions are there. They have to clean it up.

98. scire, spondere

Put the most suitable word in each space. Think about the part of speech required in each space. Make sure you use the correct form.

conscience, conscientious, conscious, science, unconscious; correspond, despondent, respond, response, responsible, sponsor, spouse

1. I'm going to walk across the country to raise money for the local hospital. Would you like to _____ me? I'd be really grateful if you do.

2. I'm pleased to say that your son is very _____ with his schoolwork and homework. He makes sure he always does it well.

3. Could you talk to Janice and cheer her up a bit? She just found out she failed her exams, and she's quite _____ at the moment.

4. The firemen broke into the burning house and found a woman lying _____ on the kitchen floor. She later came round in hospital.

5. I've sent three emails to invite Juliette to my party. She hasn't _____ to any of them, so I'm just going to forget it. She obviously doesn't care about me.

6. All the teachers are invited to the open evening. We are happy for you to bring your _____ or partner. We hope to see you then.

7. I know it's sad that I had to dismiss Jones from his job, but I have a clear _____, because he just wasn't competent enough to do it properly.

8. I've asked a lot of people to help me to complete my project, but their _____ are always negative. I don't know who to ask any more.

9. I don't think my son is really _____ of the fact that when he goes to secondary school next year, he'll have to work a lot harder.

10. I'm sorry, but I'm not _____ for any mistakes the previous manager made in this job. However, I'll try hard to put things right.

11. I've examined all the fingerprints from the crime scene in detail, but they don't _____ with the suspect's prints. We'll have to let him go.

12. One of the greatest events in the history of _____ was when Isaac Newton discovered the force of gravity.

99. torquere, turba, turbo

Put the most suitable word in each space. Think about the part of speech required in each space. Make sure you use the correct form.

contort, distort, extort, torment, tortuous, torture; disturb, perturb, trouble, turbid, turbine, turbulent

1. There is so much mud in the river now that the water has become very _____, and it's very difficult for fishermen to see the fish.

2. I've got a meeting now with a very important client. I don't want to be _____. If anyone calls, take the number and I'll call back.

3. Jones tried to take over the company's computer system so that he could _____ money out of them, but the police arrested him in time.

4. The road up the mountain is really _____, with so many sharp bends and twists that you may not see a car coming. You have to drive really carefully.

5. I don't know how Mancini manages to cope with being a football club manager. Nothing seems to _____ him. He always looks relaxed in a game.

6. The thing about journalists is they always try to _____ the truth. What they printed in the newspaper is not what I actually said in the interview.

7. If you don't clean all this up before your father gets home, there's going to be _____. You know how much he hates mess.

8. My sister has practised yoga for ten years and she can easily twist and _____ her body into all kinds of positions.

9. As the water flows through the dam, it turns a huge _____, which then produces electricity.

10. Human rights activists have protested about this government's use of _____ on political prisoners to get information.

11. Jane and Tim have a really _____ relationship. One moment they're so in love, and the next they're screaming at each other and fighting.

12. You can't understand the mental _____ that I went through when my son was so ill in hospital. I'm just relieved he's getting better now.

100. vacare, vanus

Put the most suitable word in each space. Think about the part of speech required in each space. Make sure you use the correct form.

avoid, avoidance, devoid, evacuate, vacant, vacate, vacuous, vacuum, void; vain, vanish, vanity

1. Huge deserts like the Sahara seem to be _____ of life, but there are many plants and animals which have adapted to living there successfully.

2. After the dictator died suddenly, there was no one to take over, so the power _____ led to the rise of private armies and civil war.

3. The doctor said I should _____ foods with a high salt and fat content to help control my high blood pressure.

4. I don't like women who spend so much on make up and beauty treatment. It's pure _____. I think a lively personality is much more important.

5. It's very difficult when someone you've loved for so long is no longer alive. There's just a huge _____ where that person used to be.

6. As a result of the wildfires burning in the forests, police have started to _____ hundreds of people to safety in the nearest town.

7. We had already started our meeting, when we had to _____ the room because another group had arranged a meeting there.

8. There was a strange object with bright lights hovering over my house, but then it just flew up and _____. There's no sign of it anywhere now.

9. The car broke down in the middle of this little town, so we couldn't get to our holiday house before dark. Luckily, the Bates Motel had lots of _____ rooms.

10. There was a man in the river who couldn't swim. The police made a _____ attempt to save him, as the river carried him away.

11. A lot of accountants create tax _____ schemes to enable rich people to save money by not paying tax.

12. How can you watch those awful reality programmes like Big Brother? I find the people so _____. They've got nothing serious to say.

Answers

Exercise 1.

1. navigate; 2. agile; 3. agent; 4. reaction; 5. agitated; 6. agenda; 7. actual; 8. agency; 9. act; 10. acting; 11. actor; 12. active

Exercise 2.

1. activate; 2. counteract; 3. acting; 4. actionable; 5. enact; 6. action; 7. transaction; 8. react; 9. exacting; 10. act; 11. interact; 12. proactive

Exercise 3.

1. incisive; 2. fratricide; 3. precise; 4. concise; 5. excise; 6. decide; 7. suicide; 8. précis; 9. decisive; 10. incision; 11. precision; 12. homicide

Exercise 4

1. chapter; 2. cattle; 3. cape; 4. capital; 5. chief; 6. recapitulate; 7. achieve; 8. capitation; 9. chef; 10. capital

Exercise 5

1. precipitous; 2. capitulated; 3. cape; 4. captain; 5. capitalise; 6. precipice; 7. chieftains; 8. capital; 9. decapitate; 10. precipitation

Exercise 6.

1. preceded; 2. cede; 3. successful; 4. abscess; 5. successor; 6. concessions; 7. successive; 8. concede; 9. succeed; 10. predecessor; 11. succession; 12. success

Exercise 7

1. recession; 2. accessories; 3. procedure; 4. procession; 5. recede; 6. process; 7. accession; 8. proceeded; 9. recess; 10. secede; 11. access; 12. acceded

Exercise 8

1. incessant; 2. ancestors; 3. ceased; 4. intercede; 5. exceeded; 6. deceased; 7. precedent; 8. predeceased; 9. ancestry; 10. cessation; 11. excessive; 12. excess

Exercise 9

1. closure; 2. disclose; 3. secluded; 4. clause; 5. concluded; 6. closet; 7. recluse; 8. close; 9. enclosed; 10. preclude; 11. includes; 12. excluding

Exercise 10

1. crescent; 2. accrue; 3. decrement; 4. concrete; 5. recruit; 6. crescendo; 7. decrease; 8. increment; 9. accreted; 10. increase

Exercise 11.

1. dowry; 2. rendered; 3. extradite; 4. condone; 5. donate; 6. data; 7. additives; 8. date; 9. edit; 10. tradition; 11. mandated; 12. endowment

Exercise 12

1. dictation; 2. verdict; 3. conditions; 4. contradicting; 5. diction; 6. dedicate; 7. dictate; 8. edict; 9. ditty; 10. abdicate; 11. dictum; 12. ditto

Exercise 13

1. interdicted; 2. index; 3. predicated; 4. addiction; 5. predict; 6. indicate; 7. predicament; 8. indicative; 9. vindicated; 10. indicted; 11. dictionary; 12. indication

Exercise 14

1. duet; 2. duplicate; 3. dozens; 4. doublet; 5. duo; 6. double; 7. duel; 8. redouble; 9. dual; 10. duplicitous

Exercise 15

1. disaffected; 2. effective; 3. affection; 4. deficit; 5. defection; 6. deficiency; 7. affected; 8. efficient; 9. affectations; 10. defect; 11. affectionate; 12. defective

Exercise 16

1. factors; 2. factions; 3. facile; 4. facts; 5. faculty; 6. features; 7. factory; 8. fashion; 9. factual; 10. feasible; 11. facsimile; 12. feat

Exercise 17

1. benefit; 2. confetti; 3. official; 4. profit; 5. efficacious; 6. refectory; 7. confectionery; 8. office; 9. effects; 10. affairs; 11. profiteering; 12. officious

Exercise 18

1. counterfeit; 2. infected; 3. forfeit; 4. manufacture; 5. defeat; 6. difficult; 7. perfect; 8. surfeit; 9. disinfectant; 10. suffice; 11. proficient; 12. prefect

Exercise 19

1. confined; 2. finances; 3. finery; 4. finish; 5. infinitesimal; 6. refined; 7. definition; 8. final; 9. infinity; 10. finite; 11. finesse; 12. affinity

Exercise 20

1. infraction; 2. fragments; 3. diffracted; 4. fractious; 5. fraction; 6. defragment; 7. fragile; 8. frail; 9. infringe; 10. fragmentary; 11. fracture; 12. refracts

Exercise 21

1. malignant; 2. generic; 3. congenial; 4. genuine; 5. genital; 6. genteel; 7. generous; 8. congenital; 9. general; 10. benign; 11. gentle; 12. genial

Exercise 22

1. genus; 2. progenitors; 3. genius; 4. genres; 5. engine; 6.miscegenation; 7. gentry; 8. genitive; 9. progeny; 10. gender; 11. gentleman; 12. primogeniture

Exercise 23

1. disingenuous; 2. impregnated; 3. indigenous; 4. generate; 5. engender; 6. ingenious; 7. degenerated; 8. generalise; 9. gentrified; 10. pregnant; 11. ingenuous; 12. regenerate

Exercise 24

1. nationalise; 2. nature; 3. natural; 4. supernatural; 5. naïve; 6. native; 7. nation; 8. naturalised; 9. international; 10. national; 11. renaissance; 12. natal

Exercise 25

1. digress; 2. gradation; 3. congress; 4. regression; 5. upgrade; 6. degraded; 7. transgress; 8. aggressive; 9. degree; 10. downgraded

Exercise 26

1. progressive; 2. graduate; 3. gradual; 4. ingredients; 5. progress; 6. retrograde; 7. progression; 8. postgraduate; 9. gradient; 10. grades

Exercise 27

1. grievous; 2. aggrieved; 3. gravity; 4. grave; 5. gravitated; 6. grief; 7. grievance; 8. gravitas; 9. grieving; 10. aggravate

Exercise 28

1 join; 2. conjoined; 3. conjunction; 4. injunction; 5. disjointed; 6. enjoined; 7. conjugal; 8. rejoinder; 9. joint; 10. juncture; 11. adjoining; 12. junction

Exercise 29

1. laundry; 2. deluged; 3. lotion; 4. lavish; 5. dilute; 6. laundering; 7. alluvial; 8. lavatory; 9. ablutions; 10. lavished

Exercise 30

1. levitated; 2. levity; 3. leaven; 4. relief; 5. alleviate; 6. leverage; 7. relevant; 8. elevator; 9. levy; 10. lever; 11. relieve; 12. elevated

Exercise 31

1. lieu; 2. dislocated; 3. localised; 4. local; 5. location; 6. located; 7. collocated; 8. allocated; 9. locality; 10. relocated; 11. lieutenant; 12. locale (locality)

Exercise 32

1. elusive; 2. delude; 3. interlude; 4. prelude; 5. colluded; 6. disillusioned; 7. alluded; 8. ludicrous; 9. delusional; 10. illusion; 11. eludes; 12. illusory

Exercise 33

1. medieval; 2. intermediate; 3. mediate; 4. mediocre; 5. mean; 6. media; 7. Mediterranean; 8. medium; 9. intermediary; 10. mezzanine; 11. immediate; 12. meridian

Exercise 34

1. memoirs; 2. remembrance; 3. memorandum; 4. memorable; 5. memorise; 6. commemorate; 7. memorabilia; 8. remember; 9. memory; 10. memorial

Exercise 35

1. minus; 2. diminish; 3. minority; 4. minimum; 5. minister; 6. minor; 7. administer; 8. minute (minuscule); 9. ministry; 10. minimal; 11. minimise; 12. minuscule (minute)

Exercise 36

1. commodities; 2. modem; 3. mode; 4. modest; 5. modify; 6. accommodate; 7. model; 8. modulate; 9. modules; 10. modern; 11. modicum; 12. moderate

Exercise 37

1. commune; 2. excommunicated; 3. immunity; 4. Commons; 5. remuneration; 6. common; 7. communal; 8. communion; 9. communicate; 10. incommunicado; 11. municipal; 12. community

Exercise 38

1. sever; 2. pare; 3. reparations; 4. irreparable; 5. apparatus; 6. disparate; 7. disrepair; 8. severance; 9. separate; 10. prepare; 11. several; 12. repair

Exercise 39

1. compulsive; 2. propulsion; 3. repulsed; 4. peal; 5. pulse; 6. propelled; 7. compulsion; 8. pushing; 9. propellers; 10. compelled; 11. pulsar; 12. pulsating

Exercise 40

1. appeal; 2. impulse; 3. propellants; 4. repeal; 5. expelled; 6. repel; 7. dispel; 8. impelled; 9. expulsion; 10. repulsive; 11. pushy; 12. impulsive

Exercise 41

1. person; 2. impersonal; 3. personality; 4. personifies; 5. personalised; 6. personnel; 7. impersonating; 8. personage (person); 9. personable; 10. personas; 11. personally; 12. depersonalises

Exercise 42

1. placid; 2. pleas; 3. displease; 4. placebo; 5. pleasant; 6. implacable; 7. pleasure; 8. pleasurable; 9. displeasure; 10. please; 11. complacent; 12. plead

Exercise 43

1. appliance; 2. inexplicable; 3. applicable; 4. applicants; 5. employ; 6. perplexed; 7. explicit; 8. replicate; 9. exploits; 10. apply; 11. triplicate; 12. application

Exercise 44

1. complicit; 2. duplicity; 3. exploitation; 4. complex; 5. duplicate; 6. accomplices; 7. imply; 8. implicated; 9. complexion; 10. implicit; 11. complicate; 12. reduplicating

Exercise 45

1. pliable/pliant; 2. plaits; 3. display; 4. pliers; 5. ply; 6. reply; 7. pleats; 8. pliant/pliable; 9. deployed; 10. plight; 11. replica; 12. complexity

Exercise 46

1. support; 2. supporters; 3. sporting; 4. deported; 5. export; 6. disport; 7. report; 8. transport; 9. purports; 10. importuning; 11. import; 12. sporting

Exercise 47

1. porter; 2. opportunity; 3. portly; 4. rapport; 5. importance; 6. portfolio; 7. ports; 8. portico; 9. portal; 10. portage; 11. portable

Exercises 48

1. possessive; 2. impotence; 3. repossess; 4. possible; 5. empower; 6. potential; 7. posse; 8. power; 9. prepossessed (possessed); 10. potent; 11. possess; 12. dispossessed

Exercises 49

1. apprehension; 2. comprehend; 3. impresario; 4. comprises; 5. apprentice; 6. comprehensive; 7. enterprise; 8. apprise; 9. surprise; 10. entrepreneur; 11. apprehensive; 12. apprehended

Exercise 50

1. reprisals; 2. prehensile; 3. reprehended; 4. prison; 5. reprieve; 6. prise; 7. predator; 8. reprehensible; 9. depredation; 10. reprise; 11. predatory; 12. prey

Exercise 51

1. pressurised; 2. reprint; 3. suppress; 4. express; 5. compress; 6. depresses; 7. print; 8. impress; 9. oppressed; 10. depressurise; 11. reprimanded; 12. repress

Exercise 52

1. impressive; 2. press; 3. expression; 4. pressure; 5. oppressive; 6. depression; 7. pressing; 8. express; 9. impression; 10. imprint; 11. repressive; 12. expressive

Exercise 53

1. poignant; 2. compunction; 3. point; 4. expunged; 5. disappoint; 6. punchy; 7. pounced; 8. appoint; 9. pungent; 10. punched

Exercise 54

1. puncture; 2. point-blank; 3. punctilious; 4. punctuated; 5. pointless; 6. punctuation; 7. punctuality; 8. point; 9. pointed; 10. punctual

Exercise 55

1. royalty; 2. reign; 3. regiment; 4 region; 5. regent; 6. regalia; 7. regimen; 8. regal; 9. royal; 10. rule; 11. regimes; 12. realm

Exercise 56

1. rectitude; 2. rail; 3. rectify; 4. rector; 5. adroit; 6. regular; 7. rectangular; 8. regulation; 9. erect; 10. derailed; 11. regulate; 12. irregular

Exercise 57

1. surged; 2. incorrigible; 3. address; 4. directory; 5. dress; 6. insurgents; 7. correct; 8. resurgent; 9. redress; 10. resurrect; 11. direct; 12. insurrection

Exercises 58

1. sacrifices; 2. sanctimonious; 3. desecrated; 4. saint; 5. execrable; 6. sanctuary; 7. consecrate; 8. sanctity; 9. sanction; 10. sacrosanct; 11. sacred; 12. sacrilege

Exercises 59

1. subsided; 2. assiduous; 3. residue; 4. besieged; 5. obsession; 6. dissidents; 7. presided; 8. resides; 9. assessed; 10. supersedes; 11. president; 12. insidious

Exercise 60

1. sediment; 2. session; 3. subsidies; 4. residents; 5. sedentary; 6. residual; 7. séance; 8. subsidiary; 9. obsessed; 10. size; 11. sedate; 12. siege

Exercise 61

1. insensible; 2. sensational; 3. sentient; 4. sensuous; 5. insensitive; 6. senseless; 7. sententious; 8. sensible; 9. sensual; 10. sensitive; 11. sentimental; 12. sensory

Exercise 62

1. nonsense; 2. consensus; 3. resented; 4. sentence; 5. sensation; 6. sensors; 7. dissent; 8. sensed; 9. sentiment; 10. sensitise; 11. assent; 12. consented

Exercise 63

1. signified; 2. signal; 3. design; 4. resign; 5. consigned; 6. assigned; 7. insignia; 8. significant; 9. seal; 10. signatory; 11. signature; 12. sign

Exercise 64

1. dissimilar; 2. simile; 3. semblance; 4. assimilate; 5. dissemble; 6. resembled; 7. simulation; 8. similar; 9. resemblance; 10. simulating; 11. simultaneously; 12. similarly

Exercise 65

1. simple; 2. ensemble; 3. assembled; 4. simplicity; 5. simpleton; 6. simplified; 7. assembly; 8. single; 9. simplistic; 10. disassemble; 11. singular; 12. simply

Exercise 66.

1. soluble; 2. absolved; 3. dissolute; 4. solvent; 5. absolute; 6. solutions; 7. solve; 8. resolute; 9. dissolve; 10. resolution; 11. solution; 12. resolve

Exercise 67

1. speculate; 2. spectrum; 3. spectre; 4. spectacular; 5. spectral; 6. spec; 7. spectacles; 8. spectators; 9. speculators; 10. speculation

Exercise 68

1. specimens; 2. special; 3. specious; 4. specify; 5. specialise; 6. especially; 7. specifications; 8. speciality; 9. specially; 10. specific; 11. species; 12. specialism

Exercise 69

1. respite; 2. perspicacious; 3. despise; 4. expectations; 5. aspect; 6. spite; 7. introspection; 8. expectant; 9. despite; 10. despicable; 11. perspective; 12. expect

Exercise 70

1. prospective; 2. conspicuous; 3. inspect; 4. suspicious; 5. prospects; 6. disrespectful; 7. respectable; 8. prospectus; 9. respect; 10. suspect; 11. retrospect; 12. respectively

Exercise 71

1. statue; 2. stay; 3. staid; 4. statement; 5. stable; 6. stationary; 7. stature; 8. status; 9. statute; 10. statistics; 11. state; 12. stage

Exercise 72

1. subsist; 2. assist; 3. coexist; 4. resist; 5. consists; 6. persist; 7. desist; 8. insist; 9. consistency; 10. existence; 11. persistent; 12. exist

Exercise 73

1. superstitious; 2. constitutes; 3. destitute; 4. institutions; 5. constitution; 6. substitute; 7. prostitution; 8. institute; 9. superstitions; 10. institutional; 11. constituencies; 12. restitution

Exercise 74

1. obstacles; 2. contrast; 3. destined; 4. estate; 5. restate; 6. destination; 7. obstinate; 8. predestined; 9. establish; 10. rest; 11. destiny; 12. arrest

Exercise 75

1. extant; 2. substantial; 3. staunch; 4. circumstantial; 5. constant; 6. instant; 7. instantaneous; 8. distance; 9. circumstances; 10. instances; 11. stance; 12. substance

Exercise 76

1. temporal; 2. extemporise; 3. temper; 4. contemporary; 5. temperament; 6. temperance; 7. temporary; 8. tense; 9. temper; 10. tempo; 11. temperature; 12. temperate

Exercise 77

1. attend; 2. tent; 3. tensile; 4. tense; 5. tend; 6. attentive; 7. tender; 8. attention; 9. tension; 10. tendency; 11. tendentious; 12. tense

Exercise 78

1. portend; 2. détente; 3. extend; 4. contention; 5. distended; 6. tend; 7. portents; 8. entente; 9. contend; 10. extension; 11. contentious; 12. extensive

Exercises 79

1. ostentatious; 2. intention; 3. intensive; 4. pretence; 5. intensity; 6. ostensibly; 7. intensify; 8. intent; 9. pretentious; 10. intend; 11. pretend; 12. intense

Exercise 80

1. tenets; 2. tenement; 3. tenor; 4. tenacious; 5. countenance; 6. pertains; 7. tenable; 8. pertinent; 9. maintenance; 10. tenants; 11. maintain; 12. tenure

Exercises 81

1. detention; 2. retinue; 3. abstention; 4. discontinued; 5. lieutenant; 6. retention; 7. continue; 8. entertained; 9. detained; 10. abstain; 11. retentive; 12. retains

Exercise 82

1. sustenance; 2. discontent; 3. continents; 4. content; 5. contain; 6. contentment; 7. continental; 8. content; 9. subcontinent; 10. obtain; 11. sustain; 12. containment

Exercise 83

1. terminology; 2. terminus (terminal); 3. predetermined; 4. interminable; 5. terminal; 6. terminate; 7. indeterminate; 8. determine; 9. term; 10. term; 11. Terminal; 12. determined

Exercise 84

1. terrain; 2. interred; 3. Mediterranean; 4. terrestrial; 5. subterranean; 6. territories; 7. terracotta; 8. terrace; 9. disinter; 10. territorial; 11. extraterrestrial

Exercise 85

1. tractor; 2. trace; 3. treat; 4. train; 5. trail; 6. treaty; 7. tractable; 8. treatment; 9. traction; 10. tracts; 11. treatise; 12. traits

Exercise 86

1. portray; 2. contracted; 3. abstract; 4. contractual; 5. retrace; 6. contractions; 7. retreat; 8. contracts; 9. portrait; 10. subcontract; 11. abstract; 12. abstractions

Exercise 87

1. distractions; 2. detractors; 3. extract; 4. attract; 5. subtract; 6. attractive; 7. retracted; 8. distract; 9. attraction; 10. distraught; 11. protracted; 12. detract

Exercise 88

1. viable; 2. revitalised; 3. vivacious; 4. revive; 5. vivid; 6. vitamins; 7. vitality; 8. survival; 9. vital; 10. revival; 11. convivial; 12. survived

Exercises 89

1. vocalise; 2. vowels; 3. vocational; 4. vocal; 5. voucher; 6. vocalist; 7. vociferous; 8. vocation; 9. vouch; 10. vocabulary; 11. voice; 12. voiced

Exercise 90

1. invoked; 2. equivocal; 3. convocation; 4. advocate; 5. provocative; 6. evoked; 7. revoked; 8. provoke; 9. evocative; 10. provocation; 11. invocation; 12. advocate

Exercise 91

1. colonies; 2. civilisation; 3. culture; 4. citizen; 5. civility; 6. city; 7. colonial; 8. civil; 9. cultivate; 10. civilian; 11. cult; 12. civic

Exercise 92

1. obdurate; 2. dour; 3. damage; 4. damn; 5. durable; 6. indemnity; 7. duress; 8. endured; 9. duration; 10. condemned; 11. during; 12. damages

Exercise 93

1. fault; 2. offence; 3. falsified; 4. fail; 5. defend; 6. false; 7. fend; 8. fallacy; 9. fallible; 10. offend; 11. defence; 12. default

Exercise 94

1. laboratory; 2. deliver; 3. laborious; 4. libertine; 5. collaborate; 6. illiberal; 7. liberties; 8. liberal; 9. elaborate; 10. libertarian; 11. labour; 12. liberate

Exercise 95

1. commuted; 2. mirror; 3. mutated; 4. admire; 5. miraculous; 6. permutations; 7. mirage; 8. mutant; 9. marvellous; 10. mutual; 11. miracle; 12. commuters

Exercise 96

1. prize; 2. praise; 3. appreciative; 4. expropriated; 5. precious; 6. appropriate; 7. proprietor; 8. appraise; 9. property; 10. proper; 11. price; 12. appreciate

Exercise 97

1. sanitised; 2. saturated; 3. sanitation; 4. satiated; 5. asset; 6. sanity; 7. satisfaction; 8. sanatorium; 9. satisfy; 10. sane; 11. dissatisfied; 12. unsanitary

Exercise 98

1. sponsor; 2. conscientious; 3. despondent; 4. unconscious; 5. respond; 6. spouse; 7. conscience; 8. response; 9. conscious; 10. responsible; 11. correspond; 12. science

Exercise 99

1. turbid; 2. disturbed; 3. extort; 4. tortuous; 5. perturb; 6. distort; 7. trouble; 8. contort; 9. turbine; 10. torture; 11. turbulent; 12. torment

Exercise 100

1. devoid; 2. vacuum; 3. avoid; 4. vanity; 5. void; 6. evacuate; 7. vacate; 8. vanished; 9. vacant; 10. vain; 11. avoidance; 12. vacuous